Toward the Seventh Millennium

Virtually all Scripture references are quoted from the King James translation
of the Holy Bible.

Toward the Seventh Millennium
Copyright ©1998 by The Olive Press
West Columbia, South Carolina 29170
Published by The Olive Press, a division of Midnight Call Ministries
West Columbia, SC 29170 U.S.A.

Copy typist:	Lynn Jeffcoat
Proofreaders:	James Rizzuti, Angie Peters, Susanna Cancassi
Layout/Design:	James Rizzuti
Lithography:	Simon Froese
Cover Design:	J Spurling

Library of Congress Cataloging-in-Publication Data

Froese, Arno—Hunt, Dave—Lalonde, Peter—Adams, Moody—Cionci,
Dr. John—Webber, Dr. David—Seibel, Alexander
   Toward the Seventh Millennium
   ISBN 0-937422-42-8
   1. Bible—Prophecy—Israel—AIDS—Virtual reality
   2. Antichrist

Printed in the United States of America

*This book is dedicated to the
Church of Jesus Christ worldwide.*

Contents

Introduction by Arno Froese

Toward the Seventh Millennium

T he pages of this book are filled with insight, reflecting many years of study and experience from six scholars who have gained national and international recognition in Bible prophecy and one doctor in medicine.

Toward the Seventh Millennium means the ending of 6,000 years and the approach into the next millennium, being the seventh since the creation of man.

We may dissect the world's history in the following manner: the first 2,000 years without the Law; the second 2,000 years under the Law; the third 2,000 years under grace. Thus, the next 1,000 years should lead to the thousand-year kingdom of peace.

It's important to point out that we're not trying to place a special meaning on the year 2000. One of the reasons is that we don't know exactly when the year 2000 actually happens. There's much debate among scholars regarding the exact date, for example, of the birth of Christ. Subsequently, the counting of our years could be off two, three, or more years.

Another reason that we aren't placing any particular significance on the year 2000 is that the Bible doesn't teach us to search, calculate, and analyze the years to understand or gain knowledge from the Scripture about the *exact date* of Christ's return.

The last 2,000 years, as we just mentioned, have been the two millennia of grace. During this time, the invitation of God to all humanity—to come to the knowledge of salvation—has been extended and is being preached around the world.

As a result, the Church of Jesus Christ has been and is continuing to be built everywhere on Earth. Wherever we go, whether to the north of Alaska or the southern tip of Argentina, the deep rain forest of Asia or the desert of Africa, we'll find Christians, those born-again of the Spirit of God, who trust the Lord Jesus Christ as their Savior.

Although we've been admonished by the Lord to preach the Gospel to all nations, it is He who promises the success with His own words, *"I will build my church."*

We're duty-bound to do what we're commanded. It's expected of us that we do everything within our power to obey. The Lord will do that which we can't.

The Israel Sign

To summarize, the church is being built despite its outward condition. And we have reasons to believe that the completion of the church can't be too far off. The questions regarding the basis of such reasons are answered with one word: "Israel!"

For the first time since the beginning of the two millennia of grace, the Jewish people are going back to the land of their fathers. They've established a prosperous nation in the Middle East.

That which has been unthinkable throughout the centuries, even millennia, has now become a reality and, because of that, Israel is the great stoplight for the nations of the world.

The time of the Gentiles (including the church) is running out! A new dispensation of time is ready to begin; we're racing toward the seventh millennium!

Man's Fall

We're all familiar with the Biblical record regarding man's sin against the Creator and his later separation from the living God. This happened in the Garden of Eden shortly after man was placed in Paradise.

We know, from reading the first few pages of the Bible, that man was destined to live in peace and harmony with his Creator, and in peace and harmony with fellow men and the environment.

All that changed when man transgressed the command-ment of God, and thereby lost this royal position of fel-lowship with Him.

Satan, the Father Of Lies

Who was the initiating power of this loss? Or who is the originator of sin? Satan, the great deceiver, used the serpent to deceive the woman and start the fall of man.

Satan is the enemy of God. Based on that fact alone, he must oppose God's plan. The annals of history and the pages of the Bible clearly document the success of Satan throughout the history of mankind—for six millennia.

Hate, destruction, war, and rumors of war have never stopped. However, the Bible predicts that one day there will be peace, justice, liberty, and a restored fellowship between God and His creation.

Satan knows the prophetic Word. He knows that God will establish His kingdom of peace on Earth.

Surely, he's aware that the overwhelming bulk of the world's population expects some type of world peace and prosperity to come. He also knows that he's powerless to oppose God's eternal resolution about the coming peace on Earth.

Therefore, he does everything in His power to present to man his own "kingdom of peace." That, in summary, is the battle of the ages. The Creator against the destroyer, light against darkness, truth against lies.

How wonderful to know who wins in the end! That's what the prophetic Word is all about. In the first pages of the Bible, we read about the promise to redeem mankind,

"And I will put enmity between thee and the woman, and between thy seed and her seed; it shall bruise thy head, and thou shalt bruise his heel" (Genesis 3:15).

God Is Love

Someone may now ask, "Why doesn't God simply destroy Satan? Why has He tolerated all the terrible sufferings of this creation for almost 6,000 years?"

The answer is found in one word: Love. Love can't be expressed in dictatorship; it has to be voluntary. Each person on the face of planet Earth must decide whether he wants to follow God's way or Satan's way. Men must decide whether to follow the truth, or follow the father of lies.

The wonderful message of salvation is that God has already prepared the way for man to come back. His preparation was based on love, *"For God so loved the world, that he gave his only begotten Son, that whosoever believeth in him should not perish, but have everlasting life"* (John 3:16).

However, God is righteous. He permits man to do his own bidding. The Lord even gives Satan the liberty to deceive man. If man would have been created without the ability to make a decision, then man wouldn't be a product of love but, in truth, he would be a robot. We all know that's not the case. Man has a sovereign freewill; he can say "Yes" to God or "Yes" to Satan. But one thing is sure: He can't say "Yes" to both!

Satan, the Destroyer

How does Satan deceive man? What is his strategy? How will he finish what he sets out to do? Someone may answer, "Well, it's not our business. We are saved. We have nothing to do with the Devil. Why worry about it?"

That, of course, oversimplifies the matter. Further, that rationale is not Biblical, for the Apostle Paul clearly says that we're not ignorant of Satan's devices. There's a reason for it: *"Lest Satan should get an advantage of us..."* (2nd Corinthians 2:11). That's why we should study what the Bible has to say about Satan's work, his intention, plan, and devices.

Satan's Plan

If Satan wants to establish his kingdom of peace on Earth, then we must ask how he will accomplish that goal. First, he can't run the nations without the fourfold necessities:

1. Economy
2. Banking
3. Military Power
4. Religion

The fact that Satan rules the world, including every nation, is a Biblically established doctrine. The Devil is *"the god of this world..."* (2nd Corinthians 4:4). He's the instigator of all wars and bloodshed, just as he, no doubt, inspired Cain to kill his brother Abel.

The Lord God had this to say to Cain, *"If thou doest well, shalt thou not be accepted? and if thou doest unto thee shall be his desire, and thou shalt rule over him"* (Genesis 4:7).

It was up to Cain to decide whether or not to kill his brother.

Economy and Banking

The first two of our fourfold criteria are now being established world-wide: the economy and banking. These are absolutely necessary to produce a one-world global society. One doesn't need to be an expert on economic theory to know that great parts of every country, including the United States, depend on other countries. A global interdependent economy already exists. American firms are very active globally, but that fact is equally true for global corporations originating in Europe and Asia. Indeed, it would be extremely difficult to separate global corporations into national ones.

Here's just one example: an American car may be built primarily in a foreign country, yet a foreign car, such as a Toyota, to name one, is built primarily in the United States. The one-world economy already exists, as does one-world banking.

Military Power
We saw a united world, militarily, during the Gulf Conflict, when the Allied forces, under the political umbrella of the United Nations and leadership of the U.S., successfully opposed Saddam's Iraq.

Militarily, the world isn't one yet, but this development will certainly happen soon, for the Bible tells us very plainly about the military capability of the Antichrist when it asks, *"Who is able to make war with him?"*

Religion
Not too much is said in the Bible about the economy, banking, and the military concerning the endtime one-world order.

However, when Jesus spoke about endtime events, He particularly highlighted religion. Therefore, we, too, must highlight that point. The moment the disciples asked the Lord about His Second Coming, He first warned them to watch for *deception*. Let's quote a few Scriptures to illustrate the necessity of pinpointing and exposing religious deception:

"And Jesus answered and said unto them, Take heed that no man deceive you.

"For many shall come in my name, saying, I am Christ; and shall deceive many.

"Then if any man shall say unto you, Lo, here is Christ, or there; believe it not.

"For there shall arise false Christs, and false prophets, and shall shew great signs and wonders; insomuch that, if it were possible, they shall deceive the very elect" (Matthew 24:4–5; 23–24).

Truly, the prophetic endtime scenario is marked by great deception.

False Gospel

To the Corinthians, the Apostle Paul writes, *"For if he that cometh preacheth another Jesus, whom we have not preached, or if ye receive another spirit, which ye have not received, or another gospel, which ye have not accepted, ye might well bear with him"* (2nd Corinthians 11:4). This makes it clear: There's "another Jesus", "another spirit" and "another gospel."

Who proclaims the imitation? *"For such are false apostles, deceitful workers, transforming themselves into the apostles of Christ. And no marvel; for Satan himself is transformed into an angel of light.*

"Therefore it is no great thing if his ministers also be transformed as the ministers of righteousness; whose end shall be according to their works" (2nd Corinthians 11:13–15).

These Scriptures make it plain that Satan and his angels are working to deceive mankind religiously. They're presenting another church through another gospel, producing a false Christ, or "Antichrist." Satan's servants are false prophets, false teachers, and false preachers who proclaim a false message—not the message of salvation—which will lead to condemnation in the end.

False Christianity

In this book, you'll read many chapters which specifically deal with the deception within the church. It's of extreme importance to recognize that the deception doesn't come from those movements and religions we know are the enemies of Christ, such as communism, atheism, Buddhism, Hinduism, or Islam. Rather, the deception comes from within the activity of false Christianity, which I'll call "churchianity." I would define "churchianity" as all Christendom and its activity.

Jesus doesn't say "Many will come and say 'I am Buddha,' 'I am Muhammad,' or 'I am an atheist,' but He says they will come and say, 'I am Christ; I am the redeemer of the world; I am the one who will bring you salvation.'"

That's why we concern ourselves extensively with the deception within the church.

If someone opens the Bible, begins to preach, and presents doctrines which seem identical to the Gospel of salvation, but are false, then we are in great danger of being victims of the deception.

We're not going to over-concern ourselves with atheists, agnostics, or the many other religions, because most true believers are already familiar with them.

When we hear someone preaching the Gospel, we must be very alert and act on the Bible's instructions to check, to research, to *"...reprove, rebuke, exhort with all longsuffering and doctrine"* (2nd Timothy 4:2).

Eternal Message

We're not dealing here with textbooks for educational purposes, with any philosophy that attempts to analyze man on the basis of his culture or his moral standards. Much more importantly, we're dealing here with life and death. We're dealing with eternity!

Those who are saved will be in the presence of the Lord for eternity, enjoying the center of their salvation, the Lord. But, those who are outside salvation will be, for all eternity, divided from the presence of the Lord.

The Bible says that their punishment continues forever and ever. That's eternity!

We have good reasons, eternal reasons, to check into God's eternal plan of salvation and compare it with the Devil's doomed plan of deception.

The great deception lies in the fact that the plans are almost identical; yet, one leads to eternal life while the other to eternal damnation!

In His Name

Often, I've used Matthew 7 to illustrate this point and I'm moved to do so again. In that passage, Jesus addresses a group of "Christians" who had done a tremendous work during their life in the name of Jesus. However, He rejects them by saying, *"...depart from me, ye that work iniquity"* (Matthew 7:23).

Notice that Jesus didn't identify cults or false religions, but He talked about people who obviously knew His name, prophesied, cast out demons, and did many wonderful works. And yet, they weren't His works; they were the works produced through deception, lies, and lying signs and wonders!

For that reason, I must stress that whenever you hear of a preacher, teacher, or author, whoever he may be, *deliberately seeking the supernatural,* then my warning is "Watch out! Be alert! You're entering a territory which is extremely dangerous!"

Unfortunately, this is exactly the activity of churchianity's "ministers" who, by cunning words, often using mass hypnosis, make the listeners willing tools for their experiments!

Isn't it meaningful that the Lord says to the faithful ones, *"Well done, thou good and faithful servant"* and yet He doesn't enumerate their works?

He could have said, "You have done a great job in proclaiming the Gospel; you have healed many sick; you have shown tremendous prophetic ability; you have produced great miracles in my name."

But He didn't. Why? Because *He* did it all! The only thing we're to do is be obedient.

Obedience Leading to Fruit For Eternity
Only obedience to the Lord in faith, built exclusively on the already established foundation, the Lord Jesus, will bring forth fruit for eternity,

"For other foundation can no man lay than that is laid, which is Jesus Christ.

"Now if any man build upon this foundation gold, silver, precious stones, wood, hay, stubble;

"Every man's work shall be made manifest: for the day shall declare it, because it shall be revealed by fire; and the fire shall try every man's work of what sort it is.

"If any man's work abide which he hath built thereupon, he shall receive a reward" (1st Corinthians 3:11–14).

May the Lord give you the inner joy of His salvation as you read the pages of this book and thereby produce, through His Holy Spirit, the desire to come closer to Him.

His coming may be sooner than we think!

One day, the shout will be heard, with the voice of the trump of God, *"Come up hither!"* ■

CHAPTER ONE

The Future Of Europe and the New World Order

—by Arno Froese

Summary

Many attempt to prove that the ten tribes of Israel were lost—somehow migrated to Europe—and the central and northern European nations constitute the ten tribes of Israel. This chapter shows how the Bible clearly delineates the role of the revived Roman Empire—today's modern Europe—in fulfillment of prophecy.

*B*y these were the isles of the Gentiles divided in their lands; every one after his tongue, after their families, in their nations" (Genesis 10:5).

This is the first time we read the word "Gentiles" in our Bible. They are separated by lands, nations, languages, tradition, and heritage. When the Bible speaks of Gentiles, it means all the people. That, however, changed with Abraham, the Hebrew. With this one man, God brought forth a unique group of people for a very special purpose; namely, to be a light unto the Gentiles.

The Jews and Israel

These people are commonly called Jews. Why Jews? Because the tribe after which all the children of Israel were to be named was the tribe of Judah. We also know that our Lord Jesus Christ came forth from the tribe of Judah. Therefore, the names "Israel" and "Jews" are interchangeable. When the kingdom of Israel split into the ten tribes and the tribe of Judah and Benjamin, Judah kept the identity of the name, "Israel."

It is important to point this out because many attempt to prove that the ten tribes of Israel were lost—somehow migrated to Europe—and the central and northern European nations constitute the ten tribes of Israel.

Before we go further with this message, we must clarify the identity of the Jewish people and Israel.

With Jacob, the grandson of Abraham, the name "Israel" was born. Before Jacob died, he blessed his twelve sons and we note specifically the blessing of Judah. A decisive Scripture is Genesis 49:10. Note the last sentence, *"...unto him shall the gathering of the people be."* Of course, this speaks of the Messiah in the first place, but it is also addressed to the tribe of Judah, unto which all the tribes were later gathered.

We know, for example, that the tribe of Benjamin became part of the kingdom of Judah. In some instances, we read that Judah is mentioned only, but Benjamin was already incorporated to such an extent that Benjamin lost his identity in the tribe of Judah.

Also in the kingdom of Judah was the tribe of Levi. They, too, became Jews.

A number of times in the Old Testament, the children of Israel came to Judah.

For example, 2nd Chronicles 15:9 reads, *"And he gathered all Judah and Benjamin, and the strangers with them out of Ephraim and Manasseh, and out of Simeon: for they fell to him out of Israel in abundance, when they saw that the Lord his God was with him"* (See 2nd Chronicles 11:16 and 34:9).

In virtually all of my prophetic-oriented messages, I emphasize this Biblical fact—that the Jews are Israel. Why is that necessary? This fact is fundamental in understanding the Holy Scriptures, particularly the prophetic Word. When we get confused in these matters, then many of the Scriptures in the New Testament become unclear.

The word "Israel" appears 2,565 times in the King James Bible and is definitely not limited to the ten tribes of Israel. After the kingdom of Israel was led into captivity, and from there disappeared, references to Israel still appear in the Bible through most of the books, right to the end of the Book of Revelation.

Israel In The New Testament
When the Apostle Peter preached the Gospel to Jews in Jerusalem, he clearly addressed them with *"Ye men of Israel..."* (Acts 2:22). Or verse 36, *"Therefore let all the house of Israel know assuredly...."* Thus, I reemphasize: the Jews are all the house of Israel.

At this moment, no one can definitely prove that he belongs to a certain tribe. But when the Lord comes, He will reidentify the tribes of Israel, for they will all receive their inheritance according to the prophetic Word (see Ezekiel 48).

The Gentile World

As seen from the introductory verse, we Gentiles are a divided people. We always have been and always will be. Wars have been fought for almost 6,000 years: nation against nation, kingdom against kingdom, race against race. In the earlier days of history, the wars between the nations were on a smaller scale.

When reading historic documentation on the children of Israel, we often read of kings whose kingdoms were limited to one or two cities and their surroundings.

Wars and conflicts didn't cease with man's development in sophistication. Neither did education help man avoid wars and military conflicts. In fact, during the 20th century, the most progressive scientific and technological continent, Europe, was the scene of two catastrophic conflicts which became known as World War I and World War II.

Until this very day, the nations of the world are diverse in their language, customs, tradition, religion, and philosophical ideas. Obviously, unity has been missing in the history of mankind.

The Bible, however, clearly predicts that in the latter stages of the endtime, world unity will come about. We know, for example, from Revelation 13, that *"...all that dwell upon the Earth shall worship him* (the Beast)..." (verse 8). Therefore, based on the Word of God, world unity will be established. Besides the people who built the Tower of Babel in an attempt to reach heaven, other great and powerful nations have tried to form a world alliance.

First Gentile Empire

In the Book of Daniel, God shows us that He divided the entire world into four power structures, the first being the Babylonian kingdom.

Bible readers are familiar with the great image of a statue built of gold, silver, brass, iron, and iron and clay mixed that King Nebuchadnezzar saw in a dream. Daniel, asked by the king to interpret the vision, clearly identified that the gold represented the first Gentile world empire, for he said, *"...Thou* (Nebuchadnezzar) *art this head of gold"* (Daniel 2:38). This Babylonian empire was indeed a magnificent political, economic, military and religious system incomparable in history.

In Daniel 3, we see this glorious king building an image of gold, sixty cubits in height and six cubits in breadth. This must have been an awe-inspiring work of art. Anyone who saw such a wonderful work must have been impressed greatly.

It seems to me that King Nebuchadnezzar made this image because to him had been revealed the prophetic dream which was to represent the four world kingdoms.

He received the interpretation from Daniel, telling him that one day, God would destroy this Gentile system and replace it with His kingdom, *"And in the days of these kings shall the God of heaven set up a kingdom, which shall never be destroyed: and the kingdom shall not be left to other people, but it shall break in pieces and consume all these kingdoms, and it shall stand for ever"* (Daniel 2:44).

Babylon's Own Image

Nebuchadnezzar didn't build the image using gold, silver, brass, and iron, but he put one up made out of pure gold. We must not forget that he had experienced some mighty things which no doubt must have gotten to his head.

Once the Creator of heaven and Earth had revealed to Nebuchadnezzar, through Daniel, that he was the greatest king, he confessed, *"...Of a truth it is, that your God is a God of gods, and a Lord of kings..."* (Daniel 2:47).

But this recognition apparently didn't go very far because Nebuchadnezzar only recognized the gold, which represented himself. He didn't really accept the prophetic Word which spoke of the other three kingdoms to come.

Nebuchadnezzar wanted to solidify his kingdom and his people. It was not enough for him to have political, economic, financial, and military unity, but he wanted to unite the world religiously, too.

Musical Unity

The first "united nations" proclamation that was made is found in Daniel 3:4–5,

"Then an herald cried aloud, To you it is commanded, O people, nations, and languages,

"That at what time ye hear the sound of the cornet, flute, harp, sackbut, psaltery, dulcimer, and all kinds of musick, ye fall down and worship the golden image that Nebuchadnezzar the king hath set up."

Nebuchadnezzar seems to have been attempting to change the eternal written Word of God. He didn't accept the fact that after him, an inferior kingdom would arise, and then a third, and finally a fourth kingdom. He was told that, ultimately, God would set up a kingdom which would stand forever.

He knew very well that if all people could be united religiously, the rest would follow suit. In Nebuchadnezzar, the king of Babylon, we prophetically see a picture of the *Antichrist*, the product of Satan who wanted to be equal to God, *"I will ascend above the heights of the clouds; I will be like the most High"* (Isaiah 14:14).

Six Music Instruments

It is significant that Nebuchadnezzar employed music as an element to religiously unite the people of his empire. All things were seeming to go his way. The image had been built and set up; the people had gathered; the music was played; and the "united nations" were falling down to worship the golden image.

Nebuchadnezzar had intended to change the faith of humanity, including the Jews. But there was an exception. The king was confronted by three Jews whose God he had already proclaimed to be the "God of gods and a Lord of kings." After being told of the three Jews who wouldn't worship the image, Nebuchadnezzar went into a rage. He didn't expect any opposition.

After all, he had been told by the God of heaven and Earth that he was the greatest king, and was represented by the head of gold. How would anyone dare oppose his glorious and successful system?

"Then Nebuchadnezzar in his rage and fury commanded to bring Shadrach, Meshach, and Abednego. Then they brought these men before the king" (Daniel 3:13).

Nebuchadnezzar gave these men a second chance: *"Now if ye be ready that at what time ye hear the sound of the cornet, flute, harp, sackbut, psaltery, and dulcimer, and all kinds of musick, ye fall down and worship the image which I have made; well:*

"But if ye worship not, ye shall be cast the same hour into the midst of a burning fiery furnace; and who is that God that shall deliver you out of my hands?" (Daniel 3:15). Interestingly, he enumerated six musical instruments by name:

1. Cornet	2. Flute	3. Harp
4. Sackbut	5. Psaltery	6. Dulcimer

The image was 60 cubits high and six cubits in width, and the king made sure that he listed six instruments to which the Jews should listen before falling down to worship the image. These numbers prompt one to immediately sense the spirit of the Antichrist, whose number is 666.

Identity Crisis
We must add here that the Jews were well-accepted in the Babylonian kingdom. Daniel and his three friends had been placed in leading political positions. One can well imagine that they had almost lost their Jewish identity in Babylon.

That is exactly what's going to happen in the endtimes under the leadership of the Antichrist. The greatest threats to Israel are not the Arabs, but their integration into the Gentile nations of the world.

This is also the case in the church. We already see today that Bible-believing Christianity is, day-by-day, moving closer to Roman Catholicism, which in turn is opening her arms to all religions of the world. We have to be blind not to see the reality of such a development, which will end in the one-world church!

In the beginning, the Jews, too, will participate. But then the moment will come—the hour of decision—when it will be made clear that the Jews are different, *"...a peculiar people...above all the nations that are upon the earth"* (Deuteronomy 14:2).

The three friends of Daniel were thrown into the fiery furnace for refusing to worship the image. But the God of Israel protected these men in a miraculous way. This caused Nebuchadnezzar to experience a conversion and become the greatest evangelist during the first Gentile world empire, *"Then Nebuchadnezzar spake, and said, Blessed be the God of Shadrach, Meshach, and Abednego, who hath sent his angel, and delivered his servants that trusted in him, and*

*have changed the king's word, and yielded their bodies, that
they might not serve nor worship any god, except their own
God.*

   *"Therefore I make a decree, That every people, nation,
and language, which speak any thing amiss against the God
of Shadrach, Meshach, and Abednego, shall be cut in pieces,
and their houses shall be made a dunghill: because there is
no other God that can deliver after this sort"* (Daniel
3:28–29).

Babylon & Mystery Babylon

Someone may now ask, "What has Nebuchadnezzar's
image to do with the future of Europe and the New World
Order?" Very much indeed, because the great enemy, Satan,
the father of lies, tries desperately to produce an *imitation*
that looks like the real thing.

   We have already read in Daniel 2 that God will establish
a kingdom that will stand forever. Quite logically, therefore,
Satan must find a man through whom he can establish a
world-wide kingdom almost identical to the real one.

   When we speak on this subject, "The Future of Europe
and the New World Order," we must keep in mind that the
entire world is destined to become one. Today, for the first
time in history, we have a political system which is capable
of producing this one-world order. That system is democracy. Although some form of democracy has existed since
the building of the Tower of Babel, endtime democracy will
be somewhat different.

Freedom of Religion

We must take special notice of the fourth world empire
made of iron, which is Rome. This fourth empire is the one
Daniel occupies himself with most. The second and third
empires are mentioned in just one verse, *"And after thee*

shall arise another kingdom inferior to thee, and another third kingdom of brass, which shall bear rule over all the earth" (Daniel 2:39). But the fourth empire is decisively different. What's the difference? The iron empire promotes freedom of religion.

We have just seen that Nebuchadnezzar's gold empire attempted to force a unified religion but failed. The Roman system was successful mainly because it tolerated virtually all religions. Politically, however, the people became part of the Roman Empire and subject unto the Roman Caesar.

Do we have any Biblical proof? Absolutely! All we have to do is follow in the footsteps of the Apostle Paul's missionary journeys. He went to Syria, Turkey, Greece, and Rome, and always went to the Jew first. We read in Romans 2:10, *"But glory, honour, and peace, to every man that worketh good, to the Jew first, and also to the Gentile."*

Where did the Jews meet? In the synagogue. Paul *"...reasoned in the synagogue every sabbath, and persuaded the Jews and the Greeks"* (Acts 18:4).

All over the Roman Empire, we find remnants of Jewish synagogues today, clearly testifying to the religious liberty under the Romans.

We must realize that building a synagogue isn't like putting up a mobile home or a frame house, as we are used to in the United States. The building of a synagogue was a great project. Land had to be purchased, a deed secured. Within the Jewish community, a committee had to be formed to determine the need and the financial capacity of the people.

Architects, engineers, and contractors had to be hired. No doubt, the construction of such a building probably took years. Such things couldn't have been done secretly. The Jews were able to freely practice their religion, which was permitted by the Roman government. I repeat: The success of the Roman Empire was reinforced by the Roman law, which granted civil liberty to its citizens and freedom of religion.

Romans Build Synagogue

In some cases in which the Jews were poor, the Romans generously helped, as is evident from Luke 7. We read of a certain Roman centurion's servant who was near death, and the centurion's messengers asked Jesus for healing. Verse 5 documents, *"For he loveth our nation, and he hath built us a synagogue."* Jesus testifies of this centurion's faith and says, *"... I say unto you, I have not found so great faith, no, not in Israel"* (verse 9).

Most of us have accepted the image we have received through Hollywood movies, showing the Roman soldiers being brutal oppressors, denying all civil rights to the conquered, and forcing everyone to worship Caesar. That, of course, was not the case, as our Bible clearly documents.

We must not forget that the Jews *invited* the Romans so they could obtain military protection from the enemies to the north. In the light of this fact, we understand John 11:48 better, *"If we let him thus alone, all men will believe on him: and the Romans shall come and take away both our place and nation."*

Why were the chief priests and Pharisees so concerned? Because they recognized that Jesus was doing mighty things and the people followed Him, *"Then many of the Jews which came to Mary, and had seen the things which Jesus did, believed on him.*

"But some of them went their ways to the Pharisees, and told them what things Jesus had done.

"Then gathered the chief priests and the Pharisees a council, and said, What do we? for this man doeth many miracles" (John 11:45–47).

Jesus had just raised Lazarus from the dead and there was no denying this miracle. They said, *"...this man doeth many miracles...."*

Realizing that fact, they obviously were afraid that He would proclaim Himself king of the Jews, which would mean rebellion against the Roman government. Only the Romans could install a political leader such as King Herod, the king of the Jews.

The Jews were bound by a political compromise and apparently were satisfied with the arrangement.

Roman Citizenship

Roman citizenship meant peace, prosperity, and liberty for its people, as clearly shown in Acts 22. Paul gave testimony in his defense, telling the Jews in Jerusalem about Jesus the Messiah and how he had experienced a conversion on the road to Damascus. Then in verse 22, we read, *"And they gave him audience unto this word, and then lifted up their voices, and said, Away with such a fellow from the earth: for it is not fit that he should live"* (verse 22).

National security was in the hands of the Romans and the chief captain acted according to prevailing law, *"The chief captain commanded him to be brought into the castle, and bade that he should be examined by scourging; that he might know wherefore they cried so against him"* (verse 24).

What the captain didn't know was that Paul was a Roman citizen by birth, *"...Paul said unto the centurion that stood by, Is it lawful for you to scourge a man that is a Roman, and uncondemned?"*

Again, it becomes very clear that a functioning judicial system was the law of the land.

The centurion immediately told the chief captain, *"...Take heed what thou doest: for this man is a Roman"* (verse 26).

The captain had to make sure. He interrogated Paul, *"...Tell me, art thou a Roman? He said, Yea"* (verse 27).

This Roman captain revealed that he was a naturalized citizen. He said, *"...With a great sum obtained I this freedom..."* (verse 28).

The privileged position—to be a Roman citizen—was not taken for granted.

The Price Of Citizenship

We often overlook this fact when we speak about our own country. Our immigrant forefathers indeed paid a great price.

They left behind their family, friends and relatives. They cut ties with their own nation without a reasonable chance of ever returning to their homeland.

They sacrificed their culture, tradition, heritage, and, in 80% of the cases, their most precious possession, their own language. That was the price our immigrant forefathers had to pay to come to this land!

The chief captain paid the price to become a Roman citizen, but *"...Paul said, ...I was free born"* (verse 28). And with this Biblical statement, we come to an important point in our message, "The Future of Europe and the New World Order."

The New Roman Empire

Analyzing Europe can only be done through the eyes of Rome. Why? Because Rome can rightly claim to be the founder of European civilization and laws. But not just the civilization and laws of Europe; Roman law is the foundation of the world's civilization.

This statement needs to be explained. To simplify the explanation, let's just look from Europe to the east, the west, the north, and the south.

The West
To the west, the continent of America (North and South) was discovered by a European, the Roman Catholic Jew, Christopher Columbus. The overwhelming majority of America's population originates from Europe. In the case of the United States, 87% of its people are of European origin.

I recall a conversation with Dr. Wim Malgo, founder of Midnight Call Ministry, who went home to be with the Lord in August, 1992. In answer to my question, "Will America become communist?" he said, "America won't become communist, but rather Catholic. Americans are Europeans and they must come back to their roots."

It is important to point out that Dr. Malgo made this statement in 1969, when communism was swallowing one country after another and claiming to be the greatest military power on Earth.

What did Dr. Malgo mean by his statement that America will become "Catholic?" He explained that, based on the prophetic Word, the Roman Empire must be resurrected and Europe will become the undisputed leader of the world to which even the U.S.A. must become subject.

When Dr. Malgo made that statement, the difference between the United States and Europe was undeniably clear. There was no question about the superiority of America in comparison with Europe. This was made evident by the great number of intellectuals, scientists, and engineers immigrating to the United States.

I recall a newspaper article in Australia in 1964 headlined: "The Great British Brain Drain." That report stated that over 20,000 British young men and women, the cream of the crop (scientists, intellectuals, engineers), would leave for the United States because of better pay. To show how this has changed, here are some figures comparing hourly compensation for factory workers in 1985 and 1995:

Country	1985	1995
Germany	$9.60	$31.88
Switzerland	$9.66	$29.28
Belgium	$8.97	$26.88
Austria	$7.58	$25.38
Finland	$8.16	$24.78
Norway	$10.37	$24.38
Denmark	$8.13	$24.19
Netherlands	$8.75	$24.18
Japan	$6.34	$23.66
Sweden	$9.66	$21.36
Luxembourg	$7.72	$20.06
France	$7.52	$19.34
United States	$13.01	$17.20

While these figures are not written in concrete and are subject to fluctuation, they illustrate the tendency toward a New World Order centered in Europe.

During the Clinton administration, America has experienced phenomenal growth in her economy, and the strengthening of the dollar against virtually all major currencies of the world. But the trend during the last three decades, the trend toward European primacy, cannot be reversed.

The East

When we look at the east, we notice that the Roman system, European democracy, is taking over. Virtually all of the former Soviet-aligned countries in Eastern Europe are now seeking membership in the European Union. Four nations have already been accepted into NATO.

Russia, the largest country in the world, looks toward Europe for advice and assistance. When the Soviet Union was dissolved in 1989, there was much political debate in Congress regarding a $3 billion assistance package to

Russia from the United States, but Europe had already guaranteed $83 billion!

China, still communist in official philosophy today, is practicing capitalism. In 1996, America had the largest trade deficit, not with Japan, but with China!

If we were to analyze the governments of Japan, Korea, India, and other progressive nations, we would find that they're based on the principles of European civilization. The infrastructure of virtually all nations, be it government, education, transportation, communication, business transactions, laws, etc., are based on the ancient Roman law.

For example, India, the world's largest democracy, is a British creation. Australia, a Far East continent, is populated primarily by Europeans.

Virtually all transactions, be they in politics, commerce, or banking, are carried out in European languages and based on the Roman system.

The South
South of Europe lies the continent of Africa. Fifty percent of these people speak French as their major language and 38% speak English. African countries can't communicate with each other unless they speak a European language.

Northern Africa has expressed keen interest in having closer relationships with Europe.

The countries that border the Mediterranean greatly depend on financial, economic, and scientific assistance from Europe.

From the world's five continents—Europe, Asia, Africa, America, Australia—only Europe has effectively influenced the progress of civilization.

History tells us that no African people have gone to Australia to establish colonies; neither have the Chinese gone to America, conquering the land. American Indians didn't sail to Europe to challenge the people. Only Europe circled the globe, established colonies, and influenced the development of virtually all countries.

In spite of Europe's great successes for two millennia, it has always been a fractured continent with diverse languages, cultures, and religions. Only during the time of the Romans was a reasonable unity established, but it died with the Roman Empire.

The New Europe
Although many politicians have attempted to bring about a united Europe on the pattern of the Roman Empire, all have failed.

But in 1957, through the Treaty of Rome, the European Common Market was established. The Common Market simply served to encourage trade among the six founding nations: Belgium, Germany, Luxembourg, France, Italy and the Netherlands. At that time, the Common Market comprised 220 million consumers.

By 1995, 38 years later, the European Common Market had grown to 15 nations with an aggregate population of 362 million.

When we compare Europe in 1957 and Europe today, we can trace the obvious progression toward economic, political, military, and financial unity.

In January, 1999, Europe will have to have a united currency: the "euro."

The Ten Toes
Since 1957, many Bible scholars have attempted to link the ten-toed image that Daniel reports of and the ten nations spoken of in Revelation 17:12. Scholars have said the image represents ten European nations.

In 1967, Dr. Wim Malgo wrote,

"Let us not look for ten countries being members of the
European Common Market constituting the fulfillment of
Revelation 17:12. Rather we must look for ten power structures that will develop through the European initiative but
will be world-wide."

I have always fully agreed with this statement because the
Bible speaks of "kings," not of "nations." While we don't
know at this time the identity of the ten power structures,
based on my understanding of the prophetic Word, they will
be world-wide.

That means ten power structures, politically and economically, will emerge on the planet and ultimately will be
ruled by one man who the Bible calls the Antichrist.

In my opinion, it is an error when we try to force the fulfillment of the prophetic Word by today's identities of the
nations. The only thing we know for sure is that Rome ruled
when Jesus was born and, based on the Prophet Daniel,
Rome must rule the world when the Lord comes back.

Conspiracies or Evolution?
Furthermore, the various developments of political and economic power structures in the world are not necessarily due
to certain organizations who have made it their aim to create a one-world government; rather, they are developing due
to circumstances.

For example, the progressive development of Mexico,
including Central and South American countries, forced the
United States to be a signer of the NAFTA treaty.

The same process is now developing in the Far East, to
name another example. Japan, Korea, Taiwan, and other
Asian countries are being forced to deal with the reality of
an arising new giant: China. None can afford to ignore the
economic advantages of dealing with China.

In South America, we see a new power arising, called Mercosul, which is equivalent to the European Common Market. It doesn't take much imagination to see that ten power structures will develop and could be recognized soon.

It is important for Bible-believers to keep in mind that the prophetic Word will be fulfilled. How the details are progressing are often hidden until they actually occur.

Progressive Fulfillment

Who would have thought, in the 16th and 17th centuries, that a few European immigrants would establish the United States of America, which would become the most powerful nation on Earth?

Who would have thought, even at the beginning of the 18th century, that communism would arise in Russia and dominate one-third of the world for over 70 years?

One hundred years ago, who would have dreamed of Israel becoming a nation in 1948?

Surely, no one would have thought, in the midst of the 20th century, that Europe would be united to form a political, economic, military, and financial union!

But these thoughts were sometimes expressed by politicians, economists and financial experts way in advance. For example, the Swiss Finance Minister, Mr. Feer Herzog, said the following in March of 1870:

> "The consequences of a universal currency will be simplicity of all arithmetic, operation and facilities gained for travelers, the easing of international transactions and the simplification of exchange rates.

> "When we have a universal currency, trading will receive such a stimulus that it will bypass all the trade records experienced so far."

We can conclude from these and many other unnamed developments that the future of Europe and the world looks better than ever before in history.

More Money, More Power

If you doubt it, then just check some statistics about the United States. Compare today's purchasing power for one hour of work and the purchasing power for one hour of work fifty years ago. Today, we can buy significantly more than our parents and grandparents could!

I once visited an antique car show for Model-T Fords at a shopping center in Columbia, South Carolina. With great interest, I looked at these old vehicles and had the opportunity to speak to one of the visitors, who was 87 years old. During the course of our conversation, I discovered that he had bought a car, brand new, for $735. But a year's wages brought in only $485.

Today, in comparison, a well-equipped new car costs about $15,000, reflecting an average of six months pay.

This example doesn't consider the fact that there is no true comparison between today's $15,000 car and the $735 Model-T Ford. If you were to take a 500–mile trip in a Model-T Ford and compare that car's performance with that of the cheapest car on the market today, you would quickly find out the difference.

When we make these types of comparisons with Europe, we come up with an even more astonishing result.

But there is more. Asia is arising, so is Central and South America, and even Africa. The development of these countries will cause an economic boom unprecedented in history.

I must specifically point out that success, prosperity, and peace is the *key* to the New World Order, which we see being implemented today. The Bible tells us that in the end-times, people will say "Peace, peace."

The Coming Global Peace
Obviously, people won't say "Peace, peace," if they don't experience peace. But the Bible says it will be a *false* peace, and that is in the making today.

When we look at the success of the Antichrist as described for us in the Book of Daniel, we should note some amazing statements:

> *"...he shall destroy wonderfully and shall prosper and practice..."* (Daniel 8:24).

> *"...through his policy also he shall cause craft to prosper..."* (Daniel 8:25).

> *"...By peace shall destroy many..."* (Daniel 8:25).

> *"...he shall come in peaceably, and obtain the kingdom by flatteries..."* (Daniel 11:21).

> *"...he shall work deceitfully..."* (Daniel 11:23).

> *"...He shall enter peaceably..."* (Daniel 11:24).

Therefore, in the success of the New World Order, which is being partially implemented today, lies the greatest deception of all time.

New World Religion
Therewith, I come to an important point in this message; namely, the great deception through religion. One of the major obstacles to the unification of Europe was religion.

The communists used to blame the capitalists. They said capitalism uses religion to justify wars. Unfortunately, that

was often the case: Religion played a major role in the dis-
unity of Europe.

However, this is no longer an issue. Today, religion is
rather insignificant in Europe. The tolerance for other religions, such as Islam, Hinduism, and Buddhism, is rather
high and is being successfully promoted throughout Europe.

In France, for example, there are more Islamic mosques
than evangelical churches.

Europe is opening her arms to all religions, and thereby,
we see the foundation being laid for a one-world religion.

The largest and most powerful religious/political organization in the world, the Roman Catholic Church, headquar-
tered in Rome, is keenly interested not only in the
Protestants uniting and being brought back into the fold of
the Roman Catholic Church, but also to unite all the world's
religions under the pope's umbrella.

Permit me to present some documentation for the above
statement:

> Pope John Paul II slipped off his shoes to sit quietly and
> solemnly with the supreme patriarch of Thailand's Buddhists
> at a Buddhist monastery in Bangkok...The Roman Catholic
> pontiff later praised the 'ancient and venerable wisdom' of
> the Asian religion.
>
> —*Courier Journal*, May 11, 1984, p.A7

Pope John Paul II isn't the only driving force behind ecumenism, of course. Newark Episcopalian Bishop John D.
Spong wrote:

> In the fall of 1988, I worshipped God in a Buddhist Temple.
> As the smell of incense filled the air, I knelt before three
> images of Buddha, feeling that the smoke could carry my

prayers heavenward. It was for me a holy moment... beyond
the creeds that each (religion) uses, there is a divine power
that unites us....I won't make any further attempt to convert
the Buddhist, the Jews, the Hindu or the Muslim.

I am content to learn from them and to walk with them
side by side toward the God who lives, I believe, beyond the
images that bind and blind us.

—*The Voice*, Diocese of Newark, January 1989

Speaking to Hindu audiences at the University of Calcutta,
Pope John Paul II noted,

India's mission is crucial, because of her intuition of the spiritual nature of man. Indeed, India's greatest contribution to
the world can be to offer it a spiritual vision of man. And the
world does well to attend willingly to this ancient wisdom
and in it to find enrichment for human living.

—*L'Observatore Romano*, February 10, 1986, p.5

The developing unity of Europe and the institution of a
"New World Order" and a one-world religion are not necessarily sinister and hidden diabolical movements, but rather
the natural outgrowths of our time.

Every nation on Earth always has and always will participate in this development, and during the last stages of the
endtime, they will participate gladly and demonstrate an
unprecedented unity. The Bible says, *"These have one
mind, and shall give their power and strength unto the
beast"* (Revelation 17:13).

Therefore, the question I direct to you, my reader, is, "To
whom do you belong? To a political economic identity,
which the Bible calls the 'world,' or to the Lord Jesus Christ
who poured out His blood on Calvary's cross to reconcile
the world to Himself?"

The Word of God boldly proclaims, *"He that believeth on the Son hath everlasting life: and he that believeth not the Son shall not see life; but the wrath of God abideth on him"* (John 3:36). ■

CHAPTER TWO

Virtual Reality

—by Peter Lalonde

Summary

The lines between reality and fiction are increasingly being blurred in our modern day. The role of international media and technology, especially the computer and virtual reality, are examined. Spiritual forces unlike any we've ever seen have been given liberty to seduce the world with a lie that the Bible says is so powerful, if it were possible, that even the very elect would be deceived.

L uke 21:28 has become the theme verse of our ministry. It's a simple passage: *"And when these things
begin to come to pass, then look up, and lift up your
heads; for your redemption draweth nigh."* You know,
there's a hidden prophecy in that verse. It took us years to
see it.

Let's say the year is 1865 and you live in Niagara Falls,
Canada. Let's say that this prophecy is being fulfilled in that
day. How would you know about it? You're living in
Niagara Falls, Canada, and this prophecy is being fulfilled.
Israel is back in her land and the prophetic events are emerg-
ing. How would you know it?

You might get a letter from an aunt in Asia. The letter has
come across the ocean in a boat and then is delivered across
land to you by Pony Express. By the time you get the letter,
it's six months old. And, of course, your aunt would only
know what was happening in Asia.

You would have to hope you had a cousin living in Israel
so you could know what prophetic events were happening
there. But their letter would get to you six months late as
well. So really, you would have no way of knowing that
prophecy was being fulfilled.

But Jesus said, *"When these things begin to come to pass,
then look up, and lift up your heads; for your redemption
draweth nigh."* We live in the first generation that can witness things being fulfilled as they happen, not six months
later, because of television. When something happens in
Israel, how long does it take for you to find out about it? The
next time you turn on CNN, there it is, right there on your
TV screen. We can literally sit in our homes and watch the
fulfillment of Bible prophecy.

It's a staggering thing. Yet, this simple passage of
Scripture couldn't have been fulfilled anytime before this
generation.

The Scriptures say that the Antichrist is going to arise on the scene and all the world is going to wonder after him. How could everyone even have heard of him in 1865? So, some guy named Fred in Israel gets up and claims to be the Messiah. What does that mean to the Indians living in Canada?

How World Media Is Uniting World Consciousness
But in this generation, as we saw with Princess Diana's funeral, the attention of the entire world can be captivated by the event unfolding before them on television.

Everyone watching knew the details of Diana's death. But the world wasn't just intellectually caught up in the event. It was carried away emotionally as well. This could only happen in this generation.

I could go through a whole list of events that could never have happened until this generation. The mark of the Beast is yet another thing. How could that have happened in any other generation?

I have often talked about things you see that are not real. The movie, *Forrest Gump*, depicts star Tom Hanks shaking hands with Presidents Kennedy and Nixon, and it shows him appearing on a talk show with one of the Beatles. Of course, this didn't really happen. The images were created by a computer. Clearly, Tom Hanks wasn't even fully grown when JFK was still alive. Yet, when watching the movie, you couldn't tell the two men weren't really shaking hands.

Then the movie *Jurassic Park* came out showing people walking among and touching dinosaurs. Did you know that all the acting in this movie was filmed without any dinosaurs?

After all the filming was complete, the movie was sent to a special effects house which added all the dinosaurs.

Imagine how hard it must have been for the actors to scream in fright at the sight of a dinosaur when there weren't any!

If you can put Forrest Gump and John F. Kennedy in the same room, and if you can put a dinosaur beside an actor, what is the potential for someone to deceive us in the future by using the same type of technology? Think about the possibilities.

The Blurred Lines Between Reality and Fiction
During the Gulf War, the U.S. military did everything possible to bring down Saddam Hussein. Now, I believe the Americans deliberately left him in power to counter Iran's influence, but some argue that the U.S. should have continued until Hussein was brought down.

But there is a less forceful way in which Hussein could be ruined, simply by using technology. All the military would have to do is alter some footage of Hussein so that he appears to be drinking whiskey and eating pork, both of which are prohibited by the Islamic faith.

Imagine what would happen to Hussein if this footage was played on Iraqi television. This convincing footage could be created using digital technology.

Previously, I have talked about the blurred lines between reality and fiction. When I gave that message, I had what I wanted to say all planned out, but I thought, "I'll just make it up as I go along, so about 40% of what I'm going to say will be accurate. The rest, well, it's hard to say because this stuff will just be coming to mind as I'm saying it."

You'll have to ask yourself, "Do I believe that? Yeah, it doesn't sound too bad. I think I'll keep it." Get the point?

This is a generation unlike any other before. What makes it really different? Quite possibly, the computer is the difference. You may be thinking that you don't use a computer. But in fact, the computer is the basis for virtually every aspect of our lives today. Have you bought a car since 1991? Eighty percent of the functions of a car today are controlled by a computer. Do you have a bread making machine? A clock radio? Well, I have news for you. You're part of the computer generation.

The Internet—and the Future

How fast is the computer generation growing? Statistics say that if the Internet continues to grow at the pace it has in the last three years, the number of users will exceed the population of the world by 2003. I don't know how that's possible. Of course, it's impossible.

Our book, *2000 A.D.—Are You Ready?* is the first book that my brother Paul and I have written by conducting all of our research on the Internet. We never went to a library. We never read a book. We were able to completely access all the information we needed on the "information superhighway."

You can find any information you need on the net if you know how to search. There is a bit of a knack to it, but you can just grab a couple of search engines, follow all the links, and find anything you want at your fingertips. It's information overload. It's absolutely staggering to think that there is virtually nothing you can't find. We used to have to go to a library and dig through all those reference and research books.

As a fan of the Hubble telescope, I can go to a couple of home pages on the Internet and find the latest pictures from the telescope and print them out. I can see all the latest developments right down to the minute.

Incidentally, one piece of technology that eventually will become obsolete is the television. It's too one-sided. It's not interactive like the Internet.

The problem with the Internet now is the relatively sluggish rate at which data can be fed into your computer. All of this information out there is coming into your computer through wires and devices which limit the speed of transmission.

Now, the technology is being upgraded from copper cables to coaxial cables. Compare it to a switch from a garden hose to a fire hose. A whole lot more information can come through more rapidly. We'll be able to send and receive digital information and we'll even be able to get full motion video on our screens.

But when the Internet is linked by fiber-optics, the amount of data that will be able to flow will be staggering. It will be like converting that fire hose into Niagara Falls. Get the picture? When this happens, the one-way television set will be obsolete.

Internet users can now see parts of our television show on our home page. But the image is jerky and viewers can only see a little bit because the data can't be fed through fast enough for the quality to match that of a television.

Give it a few years, though, and people will be able to sit down and watch our program over the Internet.

This difficulty with moving information fast enough is the only thing limiting the potential of virtual reality as well, which is what I want to write about.

The "Immersion" Factor

Let's say you're watching *Seinfeld* on television right now. There's Jerry and George talking, sitting in Jerry's apartment. Then Kramer comes in. You're just watching this on a flat screen in front of you, right?

But if you were watching this scene in virtual reality, you would feel as if you had crawled through your TV screen and were sitting on Jerry's couch with all those guys around you. That's what three-dimensional virtual reality is going to be like. It's about immersion.

If you play your car radio softly while you're driving, the radio probably has about 5% of your attention. While you're driving, you may also be talking to the office on your cell phone, or you may be thinking about work.

However, if you are listening to music at home with earphones on, about 80% of your attention is focused on the music. You're *immersed* in it because the music is the primary input your senses are getting. That's what virtual reality is all about. It increases the level to which you are immersed in the virtual world around you.

The virtual world, by definition, is an illusory world. It is a computer-generated illusion. If you're playing a computer game, you're not really fighting King Kong, you're fighting a computer graphic that looks like King Kong. With the flat computer screen, you can only get so involved in the game. Even if you have some speakers that give the game some surround sound, you're only about 75% immersed in the game's environment. Your wife may be talking in the background, the TV may be on, and the kids may be screaming, so the amount of attention you can focus on the game is limited. Virtual reality eliminates that.

A virtual reality system available now enables you to put on goggles and turn around and see what's "behind" you because you're not just looking straight ahead at a computer screen. When you turn around, the computer redraws the picture you see "behind" you.

More sophisticated systems would have goggles with earphones to block outside noise. They may even have a body suit so that you could feel heat sensation. There may even be a device under your nose allowing you to smell the appropriate scents in the VR world.

Let's say you heard an explosion behind you. As you turn to look, you see a flash of light and you feel heat on your back. Once you have turned around, you see that a car has blown up behind you. But really, you're just standing in a room. Virtual reality has fooled your senses into believing a car has exploded. Your senses have no way of telling the difference.

The ultimate virtual reality experience comes when you cannot tell whether something is real. If you suddenly woke up in a virtual world, you couldn't tell whether you were in one or not. Now, I'm not saying the technology is here yet for this to happen, because it's not. Again, the problem is the speed of transmission on computers.

Think about the human eye and brain, which are unbelievable. There is no computer like the body that God gave us. When I turn around, my eye rapidly focuses on the changed scenery, and my brain processes the visual information virtually instantaneously.

Computers are not like that yet. When you turn around in a computer-generated VR world, the computer has to constantly redraw the new picture you would be seeing. But it does it much slower than the eye and brain, and therefore, you feel a little off balance.

The computers know how to do it, they just aren't fast enough yet. When they become fast enough, total immersion through virtual reality will be possible.

Using Virtual Reality

Virtual reality is being put to some good uses. For example, people who have acrophobia, or fear of heights, can undergo treatment to overcome their fears using VR. They can put on the VR goggles and appear in the VR world to be standing on a ledge outside a building. They are supposedly looking down ten stories, but they know they can't really fall because they're in virtual reality. This has been a proven cure for acrophobia because it conditions the acrophobic's senses to learn that there isn't a thing to be afraid of.

Architects are using VR to design houses or office buildings. It can be used to design the layout of a kitchen or office
space. All they have to do is put on the goggles and walk
through the space in a "virtual world" to make sure it's what
they want before construction begins. It's a lot easier to
move a window or a door in a virtual world than it is to
move them after construction.

Many pilots learn to fly with VR flight simulators before
flying real planes. You can't crash a $30 million plane and
kill 200 people in a virtual world.

If you're flying a real plane, how long is it until you
encounter a wind shear? You might experience it once in
your flying career. Everyone who has used a flight simula-
tor, however, has encountered it dozens of times to train
them on how to quickly handle that emergency situation.

VR is also being used in medicine. Surgeons can practice
operations before they actually cut open a live patient.

These are all tremendous uses for virtual reality.

Technology — Not Good Or Evil In Itself

Technology is just that — technology. It's not good, nor is it
evil. It's just technology. There's no reason to fear a computer. But, like anything else, a person with an unredeemed
sinful nature can misuse the technology.

Technology can be used for good things, like practicing
brain surgery, or it can be used for evil purposes.

Computers can be used to learn how to fly an airplane, or
they can be used for violent kids' games. More are probably being used for violent video games than as flight simulators because that is where the market is.

Where the Trend Is Going

Paul and I have a computer game at home called "Doom."
I confess we've probably played that game for hundreds of

hours. It's one of the most addictive things I've encountered. You go through castles and dungeons and blow up monsters. It was the most realistic computer game of the day when it came out a few years ago.

A popular magazine reported that the average person who started playing "Doom" played over forty hours in their first week. That's compelling!

In another popular game, players fight Nazis. As you go along, you shoot a bad guy. He's only wounded, so he falls on his knees and begs you not to kill him. But, unless you shoot him, he'll shoot you. *So to continue on and win the game, you have to kill this guy who is begging you to spare his life!*

During World War II a survey was conducted because the killing rate was low. Officials were thinking, "We didn't kill enough people." The survey revealed that only 15 to 20% of the soldiers were firing their weapons. When they looked the other guy in the eye, they couldn't pull the trigger.

As the army researched further, it learned that about 90% of the guns dug up where the Battle of Gettysburg took place were still loaded. Interestingly, a lot of these guns were double-loaded.

You know how you see in the movies where the soldiers raise their guns all at the same time and shoot at the enemy soldiers running toward them? Then they reload their weapons. Well, 90% of these guys didn't shoot the first time, but they still reloaded their weapons. They couldn't bear to shoot at the guys running toward them, but they wanted to make it look like they had fired by reloading.

After researching all of this, the army wondered how it was going to deal with this situation. To that point, soldiers had been practicing target-shooting on bullseyes. But the army decided to change this and started having the soldiers fire at cardboard cut-outs made to look like people.

This was done before the Vietnam War and, as a result, about 95% of the soldiers fired their weapons during that war, just because they had been trained to shoot at targets that looked like people and not like bullseyes.

Now think about the kids today who are prepared to shoot the computer-generated guy who is begging them, "Please don't shoot me!" How much closer is this computer graphic to a real person than to a cardboard cut-out? And this is just a PC game.

What will happen when these kids can be totally immersed in a virtual reality environment? They could create a VR environment that includes their teacher who embarrassed them at school that day. When they go home at night they could blow their virtual teacher away in front of the whole class. Indeed, what boundaries will virtual reality cross?

A Venue For REAL Human Behavior?

What behavior will people display in the virtual world? Once they get a taste for killing, and the virtual world is no longer enough for them, will they take the next step and carry the killing into the real world?

One of the biggest deterrents to some of the worst sins in society is a lack of nerve. But if people gradually step into a virtual environment so that their senses can get used to violent and antisocial behavior, they may no longer have a problem with having enough nerve.

Furthermore, what kind of virtual world will people want to create? They won't create one where they are a fry cook at McDonald's. They will create something more exciting, like a scene that places them at bat in the bottom of the 9th, with two out, at the World Series. They may want to create a world in which they're the U.S. president. Obviously, people will want to be the *center of attention* in their virtual world. It's their game, right? My brother Paul has pointed out that we may be in danger of having people who never leave their houses because they won't want to leave their virtual world in which they are the "hero" and the "cool guy." Suddenly, our view of reality and interaction will change.

People watch an average of seven hours of TV a day. On average, how many hours will they spend in a VR world?

Let's not forget that you can make people react the way you want them to react in your virtual world. You can make them bow down and worship you if you want.

Paul and I used an example in our book: One of the faults with Hollywood is that often the woman says, "No, no, no! Oh...I'm glad you did it. I wanted you to overpower me." What if you create this in your virtual world and then you go into the real world where the woman is saying, "No, no, no!" Well, you've learned from Hollywood and your virtual world that this really means "Yes." You could get very confused in this world.

And what about virtual sex? Is it going to happen? You better believe it's going to happen. Pornography is the industry that drives the Internet.

On the Internet, there are "chat groups." If you're into caribou hunting, you can link up with others who are into caribou hunting. If you like knitting, or if you're a fan of a certain brand of dog food, you can chat with other people with similar interests. I don't care what you're interested in; you can link up with others who are interested in the same things!

Sex On the Internet

If you look up the most popular groups on the Internet, how many of them, out of ten, have to do with sex? Ten.

How many out of twenty? Twenty.

How many out of fifty? Fifty.

How many out of one hundred? Ninety-nine.

I set you up for that. But seriously, it's staggering that this [sexual addiction] is what drives the world.

Furthermore, we're now coming into technology that will allow the virtual world to become an environment for two or more people to interact. So I could create a multiple-person baseball game in which all the players are computer-generated, except the second baseman because my brother wants to play, too. So he logs into his computer and I log into my computer. We're sharing the same false world. Nothing is real, except to us.

This is being tested in a multiple person virtual world. Let's say you want to have a Thanksgiving dinner, but your brother lives in Germany, your aunt lives in Australia, your mother lives in Brazil, and you live in Canada. With the Internet and virtual reality, you could all put on goggles, enter the same virtual environment, and visit with each other around the table. How compelling is a world like that going to become? If someone gets cranky at Thanksgiving, you could just delete him or her from your virtual world.

Now let's look at Revelation 13:14 – 15: *"And deceiveth them that dwell on the earth by the means of those miracles which he had power to do in the sight of the beast; saying to them that dwell on the earth, that they should make an image to the beast, which had the wound by a sword, and did live.*

"And he had power to give life unto the image of the beast, that the image of the beast should both speak, and cause that as many as would not worship the image of the beast should be killed."

We are all familiar with this passage. Somehow this image will know whether we are worshipping it or not. It can speak, and it appears to be alive.

So where will this image be set up? Paris? How am I going to go to Paris to worship this image? New York? Chicago? Australia?

Perhaps this image will be found in cyberspace. Maybe this is an image that everyone can interact with through a computer. All we would have to do is put on goggles, and see the image. It will know by people's actions if they're worshipping it or not.

Now, I'm not saying this prophecy will unfold this way. But I do know that the rise of the Antichrist is about deception, illusion, delusion, and confusion. What a world in which to achieve this, a world that will exist in our very day!

This virtual world is built upon one premise: If I can create that world and go into that world and determine every detail in it, I am the *god* of that world. I can order my world however I want it. We are essentially going to end up with a globe covered with "little gods," exactly as the Bible says, in the last days.

You and I have a one-on-one relationship with Christ through our prayer and Bible reading. Perhaps the people left in the world after the Rapture will have a one-on-one relationship with the Beast in cyberspace. I'm not saying it's going to happen. I'm just suggesting this as an intriguing possibility for the image of the Beast.

A system is now emerging that is tying this world together. The world is being united. The Tower of Babel effect [the aftermath of the confusion of languages] is coming down. I can send a letter over the Internet to a guy in Hong Kong. He doesn't speak English and I don't speak Chinese. It doesn't matter because instantly the letter can be translated into Chinese. He can send me a letter that will be translated to English enroute. The barriers to communication that God instituted at the Tower of Babel are coming down.

Sometimes when I drive along the highway, I see all the satellite dishes and wonder if these are the Towers of Babel of our day.

We sit on the edge of a technological revolution that we have no idea how to deal with. At the same time, spiritual forces unlike any we've ever seen have been given liberty to deceive the world with a deception that the Bible says is so powerful, if it were possible, that even the very elect will be deceived.

How do we deal with everything coming our way? The simple answer, the ultimate answer, is by simply making sure we walk close to God. If we do, and if we submit our lives to Him, then none of these things coming upon the world will deceive us. None of these things will overcome us. God's plan is being worked out!   ■

CHAPTER THREE

A Confusion Of Purpose

—by Dave Hunt

Summary

A confusion of purpose results from an un-Biblical definition of Christian "unity." Foundational truths are discarded in favor of a false unity built upon a "generic" Jesus, and a message that won't offend anyone—Jews, Catholics, Muslims, Orthodox, and *apostate* Christians. Christian "evangelicals" who compromise the Gospel are called to account on the basis of 2nd Timothy 4:2: *"Preach the word; be instant in season, out of season; reprove, rebuke, exhort with all longsuffering and doctrine."*

John 17 records the "Lord's Prayer," a designation we usually apply to the *"Our Father..."* (Matthew 6:9–13). Of course, that's not the Lord's prayer because He told His disciples, *"After this manner pray ye."* He didn't say to recite those particular words; He meant it to be a *pattern* for prayer.

But, John 17 is specifically a prayer by our Lord — a prayer for unity. And I believe our Lord's prayer was answered.

Notice that the unity He prayed for (and which the Father granted) is based upon God's Word, upon truth, and it's based upon the relationship the Son has with the Father and the Father with the Son: *"...that they may be one, as we are."* There is no other genuine Christian unity.

Today, unfortunately, one of the confused ideas of many who call themselves Christians is that they must *make* unity. We are never told to *make* unity. Ephesians chapter 4 says we are to *keep* the unity of the Spirit in the bond of peace.

I have been charged with causing division. People have quoted Romans 16:17 at me as, *"...mark them that cause division and avoid them."*

They say that I am causing division and therefore they are to avoid me. My response is that Jesus caused division everywhere He went.

Three times in John's Gospel (7:43, 9:16, 10:19) there was a division among the Jews because of Him. In Matthew 10:34–36, Jesus says that He came not to bring peace, but a sword, and to set family members against one another. Truth divides those who believe and obey it from those who won't.

What "Causing Division" Really Is
We have to make a choice. If we faithfully follow Christ, then there will be those who will *not* follow with us.

They may call us "narrow-minded and dogmatic" and accuse us of causing division. But there is more to Romans 16:17. It tells us to *"mark them which cause offenses and divisions <u>contrary to the doctrine which ye have learned</u>; and avoid them."* You don't cause division by standing for truth and sound doctrine. You cause division by introducing false doctrine and refusing to be corrected! It is *false doctrine* that brings division into the church!

A division among those who are united in Christ is caused by something that undermines the truth that unites them. It is very clear from this passage what Jesus is praying about. He says, *"I have manifested thy name unto the men which thou gavest me out of the world..."* (John 17:6). We are not of the world. Christians are hated by the world, or should be. If we're not hated by the world, something is wrong.

To *avoid* being hated, many are trying to develop a user-friendly Christianity. Thus, Christianity is being *redefined*. A new Christianity must have a new Christ. Many are cheering Jesus, but when we check the Scripture, we find that it's not the Jesus of the Bible whom they find so appealing. That's one of the major problems today. Notice what Jesus said in John chapter 17:

"...they have kept thy word" (verse 6).

"...I have given unto them the words which thou gavest me..." (verse 8).

"I pray for them: I pray not for the world, but for them which thou hast given me; for they are thine" (verse 9).

"...keep through thine own name those whom thou hast given me, that they may be one, as we are" (verse 11).

What "Unity" Really Means

The unity that we have as brothers and sisters in Christ is based upon the unity that the Father and the Son have with

one another. Anyone who is not born-again of the Spirit of
God into the family of God through believing the Gospel is
not in the unity of the faith. It's that simple.

Therefore, when Christians try to make unity with those
who are not united in Christ, who are not united in His
Word, nor love His Word, nor even know Him because they
have not believed in Him through the Gospel, they are per-
verting and compromising the truth of God and furthering
the apostasy which we are experiencing today.

Notice also verse 14: *"I have given them thy word; and
the world hath hated them, because they are not of the
world, even as I am not of the world."*

And again, verse 17: *"Sanctify them through thy truth:
thy word is truth."*

John 17:20–23 declares: *"Neither pray I for these alone,
but for them also which shall believe on me through their
word;*

*"That they all may be one; as thou, Father, art in me, and
I in thee, that they also may be one in us: that the world may
believe that thou hast sent me.*

*"And the glory which thou gavest me I have given them;
that they may be one, even as we are one:*

*"I in them, and thou in me, that they may be made perfect
in one...."*

I suggest we meditate upon that prayer of our Lord and
upon the basis for the true unity that exists between Father
and Son and among all those who are the children of God.
Any other "unity" which men establish is a fraud and an
abomination.

Counterfeit "Jesus" That Everyone Can "Cheer"

We will refer later to Jay Gary and his book, *The Star of
2000—Our Journey to Hope*, in which the author introduces
what he hails as the world's biggest street party which he is

promoting for the year 2000 in an effort to get everybody out in the streets to cheer for a generic "Jesus" that even atheists can celebrate. In a similar way, the March for Jesus literature says it's not just Christians that they welcome, but that they want everyone (no matter what their belief) to march for Jesus.

On the contrary, Jesus did not come to this world to initiate marches, street parties and a cheering section for a counterfeit "Jesus." That wasn't His purpose and that's not what we are to do.

Pat Robertson has said a number of times that the "Washington For Jesus" rally held in Washington, D.C. in April 1980, which he co-chaired with Campus Crusade for Christ founder Bill Bright, was "a turning point in American politics." Was it? If so, it didn't turn in the right direction. America has continued downhill morally and spiritually.

Redefining "Jesus" and "Christianity"

Christianity is being *redefined* to make it attractive to the world. When we mention, by name, those who are seriously compromising the Gospel, we frequently encourage our readers to call or write to the person named.

Confronting Evangelicals Who Should Know Better

I have suggested that Christians call or write to Billy Graham and ask why his Evangelistic Association (BGEA) misused its permission to produce a special crusade edition of *Halley's Pocket Bible Handbook*. In 1962, 1964 and 1969 the BGEA produced an edition from which they *deleted everything which Halley had so carefully researched about the evils of the popes and Rome's persecution of true Christians throughout history.* Why? To appease the Roman Catholic Church? We give you the facts about that false church in my book, *A Woman Rides the Beast.*

Did you know that true Christians, because they refused allegiance to the popes, were slaughtered by the millions, for a thousand years, before the Reformation? Most people have never heard that!

The special Billy Graham Crusade editions of *Halley's Pocket Bible Handbook* eliminated that information!

Pope Innocent III, in one afternoon, wiped out the entire city of Beziers, France — 60,000 people slaughtered, women and children included. And this pope declared it was the crowning achievement of his papacy!

It took about a century to destroy the Christians known as "Albigenses," who were at that time the majority in southern France, the most prosperous area of Europe.

Hundreds of thousands of Huguenots (70,000 in the St. Bartholomew massacre alone) were slaughtered and about 500,000 fled France. Such vital information (and much more) was removed, with much effort, from the special Billy Graham Crusade editions of *Halley's Handbook.*

I think it is reprehensible to withhold such information from readers, giving them a false view of history, in order not to offend the Roman Catholic Church.

I don't know how many of my listeners wrote to Billy Graham about this. Perhaps some of you will yet do so. No one that I know of received a satisfactory explanation. They were told that such questions were not discussed.

In response to a question concerning his ecumenism, Pat Robertson wrote:

> People of faith are under attack as never before in the history of the United States of America by forces which wish to destroy all the religious values, all worship and all freedoms for Christians like you and me.
>
> We obviously have differences within the Christian faith and between Jews and Christians.

> Nevertheless, it's my heartfelt belief that ...we just lay aside certain Protestant differences to join hands to support those things upon which we all agree, such as the sanctity of human life.

People of faith? What "faith"? Almost any "faith" will do so long as one holds to "traditional morals." And Robertson lays aside far more than "certain Protestant differences" to form his coalition! Who belongs to Robertson's "Christian" Coalition? Followers of Sun Myung Moon (the Korean "Messiah" who says that Jesus failed His mission and Moon is here to complete it), Mormons, and of course, Catholics.

As long as you believe in certain religious values and stand for what's called "traditional morals," you are part of the "Christian" Coalition, even though you may be a Buddhist, Muslim, or atheist!

Here, we have not only a confusion of the meaning of the word "Christian," but a confusion of purpose. Jesus didn't say to go into all the world and join with people who have the same morals as you do and try to clean up your society. He said, *"Go into all the world and preach the gospel."* Are we going to obey Him, or not? It's that simple.

The Proportions of Ecumenism

Ecumenism is reaching staggering proportions. I have a transcript of a radio interview with Shawn Poirier, a witch. He was recently welcomed into the Salem Interfaith Council, which includes supposedly Christian ministers representing major Protestant denominations.

A newspaper article quotes a certain Pastor Wilkinson, a priest at St. Peter's Episcopal Church, who says,

> Why shouldn't we welcome a witch? We don't discriminate based on creed.

In the radio interview, Poirier claimed that there are about 2500 witches in the city of Salem. He said,

> We stand for dignity, the right of life....

The interviewer asked,

> What kind of support have you been getting from the ministers in the council?

Poirier answered,

> Oh, for the most part, the ministers are very supportive, especially in the Catholic denomination, the Episcopalians and the Unitarian Universalists. They were very supportive.

The interviewer finally said,

> Well, it sounds like you're doing a lot of good work with the Interfaith Council!

Somehow, we've changed the Great Commission into a new mission.

We are going to join with everybody who has some kind of "faith" and we are going to clean up the world.

Even witches claim they work for good and are accepted as partners in this new mission to allegedly restore "family values" to America!

Michael Green has spoken at such prestigious gatherings as Billy Graham's 1983 International Conference in Amsterdam. Many evangelists from around the world had come looking for advice from the speakers Billy Graham had chosen.

Tragically, they heard Green say the following:

> Don't talk about the new birth; talk about liberation. Identify
> and be friends with secular society; become one with them.

In his book, *The Future of Christianity*, Green suggests:

> Christians can be taught about devotion to God by Muslims or
> Hindus [who don't know God]; about the sacredness of nature
> by animists [whose god is nature]; and about goodness by athe-
> ists [who reject the only One who is good].

That all have sinned and must be born-again, as Jesus said,
is being exchanged for a humanistic gospel of self-produced
righteousness.

The Gospel Replaced By a Return To Morality

The call for a return to morality is replacing the Gospel.
William J. Bennett, former Secretary of Education and a
leader in the Catholic Campaign for America, is the darling
of evangelicals because of his stand for traditional morals
and family values. The Campaign he pursues, however, says
nothing about bringing anyone to Christ, but is all about
bringing Americans into the Roman Catholic Church — and
the leaders of that church are being accepted as evangelicals' partners in preaching the Gospel!

What Roman Catholic "Evangelism" Means

A dear brother in Switzerland, who is a leader of a group
trying to stand for the truth and against false doctrine, was
concerned about Explo '97 (held in Switzerland), sponsored
by Campus Crusade for Christ. He objected to the fact that
one of the main speakers was to be a Roman Catholic priest
named Tom Forrest, who is a leader of the ecumenical
movement at the Vatican.

The Swiss pastor shared the following story with me:

> You mentioned in one of your books, *Global Peace and the Rise of Antichrist*, on page 273, some things about Tom Forrest, which I quoted in a meeting. The sponsors of the coming conference became very angry. They claimed you had quoted Forrest out of context. Would you send me the documentation?

I sent him the documentation and the conference committee was forced, very reluctantly, to withdraw the invitation to Tom Forrest—though participation by other Roman Catholic clergy remained.

I simply reported what occurred at a large charismatic conference in Indianapolis.

Baptists, Methodists, Presbyterians and so forth attended. About half of the attendees were Roman Catholics. Each afternoon the various denominations (including the Catholics) gathered separately for their own evangelism training.

Charisma magazine stated that the Catholic evangelism training was very Biblical and would be acceptable in any Protestant church.

To refute that delusion and to show the true intentions of Rome, I quoted in the book (and the Swiss pastor quoted it to the conference committee) what Tom Forrest — in contrast to the evangelical facade the Catholics presented publicly—stated at the Indianapolis conference to a Catholic-only audience:

> Our role in evangelism is not just to make Christians...[but to] bring them into the Catholic church....
>
> Now listen again to the words of Pope Paul VI...: 'The commitment of someone newly evangelized...must be given concrete and visible form through entry into...the church, our visible sacrament of salvation."

I like saying those words, "Our visible sacrament of salvation..." and if that is what the church is, we have to be evangelizing into the church....

No, you don't just invite someone to become a Christian.
You invite them to become Catholics.... Why would this be so
important...? First of all, there are seven sacraments, and the
Catholic Church has all seven....

On our altars we have the body of Christ; we drink the
blood of Christ. Jesus is alive on our altars as offering.... And
it [this offering of Jesus] opens the doors of Paradise....

As Catholics we have Mary.... And that Mom of ours,
Queen of Paradise, is praying for us till she sees us in glory.

As Catholics we have...popes from Peter to John Paul
II...the rock upon which Christ did build His church....

As Catholics — now I love this one — we have purgatory!
Thank God! I'm one of those people who would never get to
the Beatific Vision without it. It's the only way to go...!

So as Catholics...our job is...evangelizing everyone we can
into the Catholic Church, into the body of Christ, and into the
third Millennium of Catholic history....

How amazing it is that mainline evangelicals are joining
together to "evangelize" the world with Roman Catholics by
the year 2000! How can we evangelize with those who don't
even *know* the Gospel, much less *believe* and *preach* it?

In fact, the Roman Catholic Church *anathematizes* anyone who preaches the true Gospel of salvation by grace
alone through faith alone in Christ alone.

I've quoted *The New York Times* report of a statement by
New York's Cardinal John O'Connor. He says:

Church teaching is that I don't know at any given moment
what my eternal future will be. I can hope, pray, do my very
best, but I don't know. Neither does Pope John Paul II know

absolutely that he will go to heaven, nor did Mother Teresa of
Calcutta.

This is not Dave Hunt, the critic, speaking. This is the highest authority of the Roman Catholic Church in New York!
Logically, if the cardinal, the pope and Mother Teresa can't
know whether they will get to heaven, what hope is there for
the average Catholic? Is this just the cardinal's opinion? No,
he says it is the official church teaching!

Mother Teresa received the praise of evangelicals for
standing up to the Clintons and speaking out against abortion at the 1993 Presidential Prayer Breakfast. But let me tell
you what else she said at that breakfast:

> One of the most demanding things for me is traveling every-
> where and with publicity. I have said to Jesus that if I don't go
> to heaven for anything else, I will be going to heaven for all the
> traveling, with all the publicity, because this purifies me and
> sanctifies me and makes me really ready to go to heaven.

That's tragic! Mother Teresa had no real hope of heaven,
was not trusting in the finished work of Christ on the cross,
but in her own good deeds and suffering and in the sacraments of her church. As a good Catholic, she prayed the
Rosary constantly for her salvation.

This is all because the official teaching of the Catholic
Church is that no one can know whether they will get to
heaven or not — and if they do, *it will be through the sacraments of the church and their own works.* Nearly one billion
souls are relying upon this false Catholic "gospel!"

The "Orthodox" Way to Heaven
I recently stood in an Orthodox church in Romania. The
head priest, a very friendly man, showed me the pictures of

their "saints" and the various icons, which are supposed to be windows to heaven. I acted like the earnest Philippian jailer and asked,

"Sir, what must I do to be saved? How can I get to heaven? I really want to know."

He replied, "You must pray."

I asked, "How much do I have to pray?"

"You must pray a lot," he said.

"But how much?" I repeated.

"You must pray everywhere you go, every day, all day long. You must pray and pray," he told me.

I asked, "Will I ever know when I've prayed enough?"

"No," he replied, "you can never pray enough."

"But," I implored, "can I ever know that I'm going to get to heaven?"

His answer was final: "No, you can never know whether you will get to heaven. The idea that you can know comes from sects like Baptists. But the official teaching of the Orthodox Church is that you can never know!"

Again, how tragic!

A recent census in Romania revealed that 90% of the people are Orthodox. And the census lists two categories of Orthodox: believers and atheists. You can be Orthodox and at the same time be an atheist! Under communism, you could be a member of the Communist Party yet remain "Orthodox."

What one believes matters little (as in Catholicism) so long as one looks to the church for salvation—and the church can give no assurance, which keeps the people in bondage to its priests and rituals.

Frankie Schaeffer (son of Francis and Edith), in his book, *Dancing Alone* (which tells of his conversion to Orthodoxy), calls being born-again with assurance of heaven the evangelical's "magic silver bullet." He admits that he had to throw away all of the evangelical faith that his famous parents had taught him in order to become Orthodox. He says you can't know whether you will ultimately be saved.

Orthodoxy is a *works trip* in bondage to the church. Evangelicals can no more join with them in "evangelizing the world" than with Roman Catholics!

Orthodoxy and Catholicism have few differences and both preach a false gospel of salvation by works and ritual through the church.

No Need For Orthodox Or Catholic "Hardware"

If you have believed the Gospel of Jesus Christ, you don't need articles of religious hardware such as Orthodox icons or the Roman Catholic scapular (which promises that whoever dies wearing it shall not suffer eternal fire) as your hope of heaven. Anyone who relies upon such objects or promises is not believing the Gospel.

Pope John Paul II says, "I have worn a scapular since I was a child."

It is clear, then, that he is trusting in Christ, plus a scapular. But to trust in Christ plus anything is to *reject* Christ!

Ask for a Mass Card at any mortuary. It says,

> With the sympathy of [you fill in your name] the sacrifice of the Mass will be said for the repose of the soul of [fill in the name of the deceased].

The Mass Card is then given with an offering to the priest. He will put it on the altar (one time) when he says Mass and that will supposedly reduce the time of suffering in purgatory for the person named.

How much purgatory will be shortened is unspecified. Even the pope doesn't know how many Masses may be needed to get the deceased out of purgatory and finally into heaven. So Mass after Mass is said in the hope that one of them will finally open heaven's door.

The father of a friend of mine died some months ago and more than $2,000 in Mass Cards were purchased at the funeral for the repose of his soul. That is Roman Catholicism today, not just back in the Dark Ages!

The Folly Of Joining With Catholicism's False Gospel
How, then, can any evangelical join in partnership with this false religion? Yet many evangelical leaders are stating that the Roman Catholic Church teaches the true Gospel!

I'm going to shock you a little more. Please don't get angry with me for telling you the facts, even if you would rather not hear them.

Ads in newspapers and magazines across the country offer videos of talks by now-deceased Archbishop Fulton J. Sheen, who was the nearest thing to a televangelist that the Catholic Church ever had.

Bishop Fulton Sheen's Apostasy
In *A Woman Rides the Beast,* I quote Sheen to the effect that, as a young priest, he vowed to offer a Mass in Mary's honor every Saturday, and that he had made 30 pilgrimages to Our Lady of Lourdes in France and ten pilgrimages to Our Lady of Fatima in Portugal.

He said that he, therefore, had confidence that when he appeared before Him, Christ would say, "I heard my mother speak of you."

That was Sheen's hope of heaven and part of the gospel he preached! Yet, Billy Graham called him a dear friend who truly lived the Christian life!

And the ads for Sheen's videos contain this endorsement signed by Billy Graham:

> Bishop Sheen was the greatest communicator of the twentieth
> century.

Yes, Sheen was a great communicator, but he preached a
false gospel that will leave any who believe it in *hell*!

But, Billy Graham's *endorsement* causes many to listen
to it and to heed it to the loss of their souls.

Write to Billy Graham and ask him why he would
endorse this man's video sermons which present the false
gospel of Catholicism.

Billy Graham needs to be accountable for what he says
and does just as you and I must be accountable also.

Where the Ecumenical Movement Is Leading

The extent of the ecumenical movement and the accompa-
nying delusion are staggering.

The pope has had five meetings with Yasser Arafat, a terrorist, murderer and liar. Arafat told reporters that he had
invited the pontiff to celebrate Christmas in Bethlehem in
the year 2000 and the pope had accepted his invitation.
Arafat said,

> I have offered to His holiness the invitation to celebrate with
> us the 2,000th year of our Jesus Christ.

Our Jesus Christ? What a fraud! Islam teaches that Christ is
not God, is *not* the Savior, and that rather than dying in *our*
place, someone [Ishmael] died in *His* place.

If you visited Israel, you would see a number of verses
from the *Qur'an* inscribed in Arabic inside the Dome of the
Rock. One of them reads,

*Allah is not a father and he has
no son.*

This is not the God of the Bible. This is not the God of Abraham, Isaac and Jacob as Jesus described God, but a god who hates Jews and wants them all destroyed.

In fact, the *Qur'an* calls for the death of all infidels (non-Muslims) in Islam's conquest of the world. Islam is a false religion of fear, bloody conquest, and salvation through works.

Schuller and the Pope Legitimize Islam

Yet, Robert Schuller says that if he returned 100 years from now and found that his descendants were all Muslims, it wouldn't bother him so long as they weren't atheists.

The pope, too, whom Schuller admires, goes along with Islam and even with Palestinian Authority President Yasser Arafat, whose hatred of Jews and determination to exterminate them is the product of Islam.

The Drive To Global Ecumenism: A False Unity

We are experiencing an astonishing ecumenism, a false unity which the pope and even many evangelical leaders and movements such as Promise Keepers are seeking to establish by the year 2000. This is a *confusion of purpose*.

Denial of The Faith By "Christian" Leaders

It is shocking when the denial of faith is coming from those who have been looked up to and honored as church leaders.

The late Norman Vincent Peale was one of the best known and most widely honored Christian leaders. His heresies are no secret, but he publicly flaunted them for decades.

He denied that the virgin birth of Christ was essential, and said that God is a force we can tap into. On the *Phil Donahue Show* in 1984, Peale made the following remark which showed how heretical his "gospel" was:

> It's not necessary to be born-again. You have your way to God,
> I have mine. I found eternal peace in a Shinto shrine...God is
> everywhere.

Donahue was shocked and challenged Peale:

> But you're a Christian minister. You are supposed to tell me
> that Christ is the way, the truth and the life, aren't you?

Peale replied,

> Christ is one of the ways; God is everywhere.

Instead of being denounced, Peale was praised by evangel-ical leaders. Robert Schuller honored him as his personal mentor. Billy Graham said,

> I know of no one who has done more good for the cause of
> Christ and for the kingdom of God than Ruth and Norman
> Peale.

I can't think of anyone who has done more *harm* for the cause of Christ! Graham may try to excuse himself by say-ing that he's not called to bring correction to the church—though the Bible puts that responsibility upon all who preach God's Word. However, he surely isn't called by God to praise and commend those who lead others astray!

Robert Schuller not only calls Norman Vincent Peale his "mentor"; he also claims to be the mentor of Bill Hybels of Willow Creek Community Church near Chicago, which is said to be the model of a church for the next century.

Billy Graham takes credit for persuading Schuller to get his message on TV and even told him to call his program *The Hour of Power*. Graham appeared on the 1000th *Hour*

of Power along with other outstanding "Christians" such as
Bob Hope and Sammy Davis, Jr. to praise Schuller!

The Infamous Graham Interview On Larry King Live

After Billy Graham prayed his rather generic prayer at the
inauguration of President Clinton in January 1997, he
appeared again on the *Larry King Live* show, where he has
frequently been a guest. I'm quoting from the transcript:

> Larry King: What do you think of other [he gropes for the
> word]...like Mormonism, Catholicism, and other faiths within
> the Christian context?
> Billy Graham: Oh, I think I have a wonderful fellowship
> with all of them. For example...[King interrupts].
> King: You're comfortable with Salt Lake City? You're
> comfortable with the Vatican?
> Graham: I'm very comfortable with the Vatican. I've been
> to see the pope several times. In fact, the day he was inaugu-
> rated [made pope]...I was preaching in his cathedral in
> Krakow. I was his guest. And when he was over here in
> Columbia, South Carolina, he invited me on the platform to
> speak with him. I would give one talk and he would give the
> other. But I was two-thirds of the way to China.
> King: You like this pope?
> Graham: I like him very much.... He and I agree on almost
> everything.
> King: Are you...are you comfortable with Judaism?
> Graham: Very comfortable.... Yitzhak Rabin was a great
> friend...[and] in New York, they have had me to the
> Rabbinical Council to meet with them and to talk with them,
> and Rabbi Tannenbaum, who was a great friend of all of us,
> who died, he gave me more advice and more counsel, and I
> depended on him constantly, theologically and spiritually and
> in every way....

King: Mr. Graham, if you had 30 seconds during the half-time at the Super Bowl, what would you tell the audience?

Graham: I would tell them to...think about another game...the game of life, and to be sure they're on God's side, that God loves them and God is interested in them, and they can pray to God, and He'll answer their prayers.

How pathetic it was to give this insipid "gospel" on the *Larry King Live* show and to propose it for halftime at the Super Bowl! There was no Christ, no Cross, no Gospel and no salvation. Graham has faithfully preached the Gospel in his crusades, but at other times when he had the opportunity to reach an even larger audience, he has compromised.

The Ecumenical Road To False Unity

Can anyone imagine Jesus or the Apostle Paul saying that the rabbinical councils invited them to speak and that Jesus or the Apostle Paul had relied on some rabbi "...theologically and spiritually, and in every way"?

And to agree with the pope on almost everything, when the differences between the Biblical Gospel that saves and the Roman Catholic gospel that damns are as great as the distance between heaven and hell?

There can be no doubt that Billy Graham has been *the* leader in bringing us to the present ecumenical delusion!

When Robert Schuller interviewed Billy Graham on his program more recently, he reminded Graham,

You know, you started this program. You're the one who told me to get on television. You even named it. You called it *The Hour Of Power*. "Well, I'm honored," replied Billy.

And what is Schuller's message that Graham praises so highly? Let me quote him from memory:

> What sets me apart from fundamentalists, who are always try-
> ing to convert people to believe like they do...is that we know
> the things the major faiths can agree upon. We try to focus on
> those without offending those with different viewpoints, or
> without compromising my own Christian commitment.

Almost everyone knows that the religions of the world don't
even agree on who God is, and they certainly don't agree on
the Gospel. They don't agree on Jesus Christ.

They don't agree on anything of importance.

If Schuller is going to preach only those things which the
great religions agree upon, his lips will be sealed.

But that's the man Billy Graham often praises and to
whom he said,

> You ought to get your message on TV. God bless you for many
> more years of *The Hour Of Power*.

Schuller must be a master at telling everyone what they
want to hear, because he told Billy Graham that:

> ...Thousands of pastors, and hundreds of rabbis, and...over a
> million Muslims a week watch [Schuller's program]...

Imagine giving a message that appeals equally to pastors,
rabbis and Muslims and doesn't challenge the "faith" of any
of them! Schuller then said to Graham,

> This is your platform. You started *The Hour Of Power*. You got
> me into this. Now have the last word. Give them a message
> right from your heart!

Once again there was the same compromise as on the Larry
King program. Graham said:

> Well, the message is that God loves you. Whoever you are,
> wherever you are, whatever your religious background. God
> loves you, He wants to come into your heart and change the
> direction of your life and give you a peace and a joy that
> you've never had before. And He will do that today, if you will
> make that commitment to Him.

No Christ, no Cross, no Gospel, no salvation, but a generic "God" that any religion could accept. How tragic!

We are not trying to indict Billy Graham for never having preached the Cross because he has.

We give these quotations to show the extent of the compromises being made by evangelical leadership and to illustrate the fact that we are entering a period of time which the Bible calls the "apostasy." It is marked by an ecumenical movement such as the world has never seen in preparation for the Antichrist and his world government and world religion. We are witnessing a *redefining* of the Gospel and an unwillingness to stand firm for truth. A secular writer recently wrote:

> Christianity is now fully politicized. The Catholic bishops and
> Ralph Reed [former head of Pat Robertson's Christian
> Coalition] have no trouble speaking about the importance of
> pro-family legislation, but they are reluctant to lay out such
> basics as the Christian teaching on salvation.

The longer the process of politicization continues, the thinner the faith gets. Political ambition has caused people to water down their beliefs for the sake of gaining favor.

The first stage of the sellout comes with exaltation of *political pluralism* above *doctrinal truth*.

The second stage is marked by a *denial of doctrinal truth* in favor of *achieving political goals*.

The deeper our involvement in political and social action becomes, the more we lose sight of the Great Commission: the preaching of the Gospel.

For example, if I'm protesting at an abortion clinic, I have a Catholic on one side, a Mormon on the other and a Moonie close by. We are all working against abortion and all those other things which Christians ought to oppose.

But this is a false and manufactured unity which is contrary to the unity we have in Christ! I can't share the Gospel with those working with me because they would be offended and it would break up the so-called "Christian Coalition."

Promise Keeping

In a major Catholic newspaper, *Our Sunday Visitor* (July 20th, 1997), the front cover and two-page feature article were about Promise Keepers. The paper reported,

> At its March meeting, Promise Keepers' Board of Directors welcomed Mike Timmis as a new member...a longtime leader in the Catholic Charismatic Movement.

> At several rallies this year, Promise Keepers has spotlighted Catholic evangelist Jim Berlucchi.

> In June, Promise Keepers hosted a Catholic Summit at its headquarters.
>
> Earlier this year, Promise Keepers amended its statement of faith, revising the lines that Catholics had found offensive.

Bill McCartney (Promise Keepers founder) told *Our Sunday Visitor* that:

> Full Catholic participation was our intention from the start.

No distinction is made between evangelicals and Catholics. Both are *assumed* to be saved.

Promise Keepers is not a new movement. Its first meeting was held at the base of Mt. Sinai 3,500 years ago. God gave Israel Ten Commandments which the Israelites all promised to keep. There is nothing wrong with the Ten Commandments. The problem is that we can't keep them.

Then, what good will the seven new promises of Promise Keepers do? And by what authority are these now being imposed upon the church as the secret to living a fruitful and victorious Christian life?

One of the seven newly-invented promises requires each man attending PK rallies to go back and support his church. Catholics are to give their full support to their churches. Protestants who come from apostate denominational churches are to go back and support their churches as well. No one is to be told that anything is wrong. This is un-Biblical ecumenism.

Promise Keepers has no doubt been a help to many men. Souls have been saved and lives changed for the better. But there are also serious problems that need to be acknowledged and addressed by its leaders.

A Confusion Of Purpose

There is a *confusion of purpose* that attempts to make a false unity with those who are not one in Christ and with the Father. Those who preach a false gospel that damns the soul are not reproved but are embraced as brothers in Christ and full support is given to apostate churches.

This false unity is being promoted by some of the leading evangelicals and it will play into the hands of the coming Antichrist. May the Lord help us to recognize the error very clearly and to stand firmly for the unchanging truth of God! ■

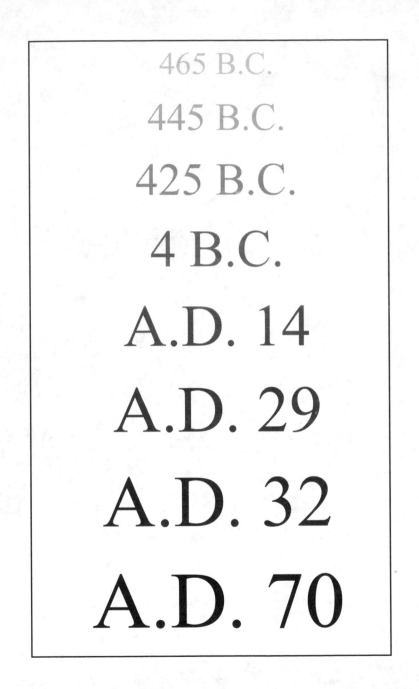

465 B.C.

445 B.C.

425 B.C.

4 B.C.

A.D. 14

A.D. 29

A.D. 32

A.D. 70

CHAPTER FOUR

A Confusion Of Dates

—by Dave Hunt

Summary

Our title implies that dates cause confusion. Yet, the Bible gives us several firm dates that help us determine the fulfillment of Bible prophecy. This chapter gives us the fascinating details on dates that have been clearly vindicated. Other events are intended to occur without the knowledge of an exact date. This chapter gives us a solid Biblical background on when and when not to use dates in our Bible exposition.

Setting dates for the Rapture has been a popular endeavor. You remember the book, *88 Reasons Why the Rapture Could Occur in 1988*. Then it was 89 Reasons for '89. Then somebody predicted the Rapture for the year 1994, then 1996. Many dates have been set with great expectation, yet all have passed without the promised Rapture of the church—and very often without the date-setters seeing or admitting their error.

The Bible Provides Dates

There is no doubt, however, that the Bible does give dates. As far as I know, two dates are clearly set forth in the Bible.

First of all, we find the date when the command was given to rebuild Jerusalem in Nehemiah, chapter two. It's a very important date. Nehemiah tells us it was in the twentieth year of Artaxerxes.

Historians say he ruled from 465 B.C. to 425 B.C., so the twentieth year of his reign would be 445 B.C. Nehemiah tells us also that it was in the month of Nisan. When the day of the month is not given, it means the first day. So we have a date: Nissan first, 445 B.C.

Why is this date so important that the Bible gives it to us? Its significance is explained in Daniel 9:24–26. The angel Gabriel tells Daniel that from the going forth of the commandment to rebuild Jerusalem (which Nehemiah received from Artaxerxes Longimanus) until the coming of Messiah the Prince would be "69 weeks of years."

If you calculate it out according to the 360–day year of the Jews and Babylonians, it brings you to April 6, A.D. 32. That was the day we now celebrate as Palm Sunday when Jesus rode into Jerusalem on the donkey—483 years or 69 weeks of years to the *day* from the date that Artaxerxes gave Nehemiah the authority to rebuild Jerusalem! (Not the Temple, which had already been rebuilt, but Jerusalem.)

No one can dispute the fact that this is when the Messiah was to be recognized by Israel—a fact which ought to convince the Jews that the Messiah has already come.

If Jesus, who was hailed as the Messiah on that very day—as he rode into Jerusalem on a donkey in fulfillment of prophecy—was not the Messiah, then who was? Tragically, the Jews of Jesus' day didn't know that prophecy, or they would have been watching for their Messiah on that very day and on that basis alone would have concluded that Jesus was the Messiah of Israel promised by their prophets.

Instead, after hailing him as the Messiah (because of the recent resurrection of Lazarus after four days in the grave), they demanded that Pilate crucify Him, again, exactly as the prophets had foretold.

Another date closely related to Daniel's prophecy is given to us. Daniel told us when the Messiah was to come. But how do we know for certain that Jesus was even on the Earth at that special time? Luke gives us a date which demonstrates that vital fact.

Luke 3:1–2 states: *"Now in the fifteenth year of the reign of Tiberius Caesar, Pontius Pilate being governor of Judaea, and Herod being tetrarch of Galilee, and his brother Philip tetrarch of Ituraea and of the region of Trachonitis, and Lysanias the tetrarch of Abilene,*

"Annas and Caiaphas being the high priests, the word of God came unto John the son of Zacharias in the wilderness."

Some wonder why these verses are even there. It sounds like the "begats" and "begottens" in The Old Testament. What's the point? You may be certain that the Holy Spirit makes no mistakes and that every word is important in God's purposes for our understanding. In fact, through these names of persons and places, this vital date is established.

By the way, there's a well-publicized group called "The Jesus Seminar," made up of so-called theologians. I remember debating Dr. Robert Funk, the group's leader, on secular radio. One of the first things I said was,

"Bob, I'm sorry, you were born 1900 years too late! We have the record of eyewitnesses who were actually there—and I can prove it. You weren't there. So who are you to tell us what did or did not happen back then and what Jesus said or didn't say? On what basis can you contradict those who were there?"

How do we know we have the record of eyewitnesses? Well, we deal with that question in some depth in my book, *In Defense of the Faith*. The verses we've just read are part of the proof God has given us in His Word.

We have a date: the fifteenth year of the reign of not just any Caesar but of Tiberius Caesar. We are told the names of men who held technical offices at that time (Caesar, governor, tetrarch and high priest) and the places where they fulfilled these precise functions.

You would have had to be an eyewitness to have known this information. You couldn't have written it centuries later as "The Jesus Seminar" claims.

Can you remember who was the mayor of your town 20 years ago, 30 years ago, or of the adjoining towns 40 years ago? Who was the pastor of the church down the street even 10 years ago? You probably can't remember. And what kind of records would you have to consult even today in order to obtain such information?

The Bible account is accurate and it has taken years of archaeological effort to verify the facts—facts which could only have been provided by eyewitnesses.

There are, however, some apparent problems. You may be certain that the skeptics and critics have gone through the Bible with a microscope and they have found seeming discrepancies that most Christians have overlooked. In this passage there are two of these.

What Is the Truth About Alleged Bible Dating Discrepancies?

Historians tell us that Tiberius succeeded Augustus. Luke chapter 2 says, *"And it came to pass in those days, that there went out a decree from Caesar Augustus, that all the world should be taxed."* So at least the Bible got that right—Augustus preceded Tiberius. And therein we have the solution to one of the problems.

Historians agree that Tiberius began to reign in A.D. 14. Thus, the fifteenth year of his reign would be A.D. 29. Verse 23 tells us that at that date Jesus *"...began to be about 30 years of age."* So, He must have been 29, going on 30, in A.D. 29. He must, therefore, have been born in 0. That's where the calendar comes from, and it's wrong. The so-called Christian world is looking forward to the year 2000, supposing it to be the 2000th birthday of Jesus. Wrong.

We know from Matthew that Jesus was born in the days of Herod the Great, and Herod died in 4 B.C. So we have an apparent contradiction between Matthew and Luke. However, Will Durant, in his *Story of Civilization*, writes that in A.D. 9, the citizens of Rome were very angry because, although Augustus was still technically ruling, he was so elderly and ill that Tiberius had already begun to rule in his place.

So, the fifteenth year of his reign would have been A.D. 24 and if Jesus was 29 at that point He must have been born about 5 B.C. and that would have been in the days of Herod the Great as Matthew tells us.

Critics, however, have noted another problem. Luke 2:2 says, *"And this taxing was first made when Cyrenius was governor of Syria."*

Thus, he was governor of Syria when Jesus was born. But historians claimed that Cyrenius governed Syria from A.D. 6 to 20. So Jesus couldn't have been born before A.D. 6 according to this data, and on that basis critics declare the Bible unreliable.

In fact, archaeologists dug up additional information which indicated that Cyrenius had been governor of Syria *twice*: the first time from about 6 B.C. to 1 B.C. So Jesus, as the Bible says, was indeed born when Cyrenius was governor of Syria. The Bible's accuracy not only here but in many other places proves that it could only have been written by eyewitnesses. The point I'm trying to make, however, is that the Bible does give us some very important dates.

Matthew and Luke establish that Jesus was on the Earth at the right time to ride into Jerusalem on that donkey in fulfillment of the prophecy, *"Rejoice greatly, O daughter of Zion; shout, O daughter of Jerusalem: behold, thy King cometh unto thee: he is just, and having salvation; lowly, and riding upon an ass, and upon a colt the foal of an ass"* (Zechariah 9:9).

Daniel gives us one of the most important prophecies in the Bible, and Luke provides proof that Jesus was on the Earth at the right time to fulfill it. This is something to share with your Jewish or skeptical non-Jewish friends. The Messiah has already come, precisely 69 weeks of years after the command to rebuild Jerusalem, so it makes no sense for Jews to await the first appearance of Messiah. Nor can skeptical non-Jews explain away the fact that Jesus fulfilled this prophecy and dozens of others, something which couldn't have happened by chance.

Reason For Unbelief: Failure To Study Prophecy
Failure to study prophecy and to take it seriously prevents many from believing in Christ.

And as a result, the world will embrace the Antichrist.

A pastor friend of mine took a group to Israel recently. A couple of young men from his church went into a synagogue and talked with a rabbi. They told him, "We're followers of Jesus. We believe that He is the Messiah promised by Hebrew prophets in the Bible."

The rabbi said, "Well, we don't believe that. We believe that the Messiah is yet to come."

So the two young men asked a logical question: "How will you recognize him when he appears?"

They were shocked to hear the rabbi's very Biblical description of the Antichrist. He said, "He will be a great world leader who will bring peace to the Middle East and to the world. And he doesn't have to be Jewish."

Interesting! The Jews are still confused about when the Messiah was to come. If they would look at the Scriptures, they would find a clear answer. It's quite plain, both in The Old Testament and in The New Testament, that the Messiah had to come *twice*. Right? You couldn't put into one event and one time frame what The Old Testament said about the Messiah's coming. That fact confused the disciples and the rabbis.

Remember, when Jesus was on the Cross, the rabbis mocked Him. They thought they had proven He wasn't the Messiah by nailing Him to the Cross. They didn't understand that the Messiah had to be crucified, because they only were able to believe what the prophets had said about Him establishing a kingdom, not what they had said about His death for our sins.

In fact, had Jesus not been crucified, He wouldn't have been the Messiah! The prophets said He would be crucified, and they foretold that hundreds of years before crucifixion was known. But the disciples didn't understand that. Remember, the two on the road to Emmaus were very disheartened. They had thought that Jesus was the Messiah because of His life and teaching and miracles, but His crucifixion seemed to prove that He wasn't the Messiah after all.

In Matthew 24:1 we read, *"And Jesus went out and departed from the Temple: and his disciples came to him for to shew him the buildings of the Temple."* Wait a minute! Jesus is God. The Temple was built for Him. And they thought He would be impressed?

"And Jesus said unto them, See ye not all these things? Verily I say unto you, there shall not be left here one stone upon another, that shall not be thrown down." The disciples were stunned. Should they have been? No. They should have said, "Praise God, you must be the Messiah!"

Why would they say that? Because Daniel 9 very clearly says that the Messiah would come and then the city and the sanctuary (Temple) would be destroyed by the people of the Prince who would come (the Antichrist) who must be of the Roman Empire, because it was the Roman armies that destroyed Jerusalem and the Temple.

So, if Jerusalem and the Temple were not going to be destroyed right after Jesus came, then He wasn't the Messiah. Do you see the importance of understanding prophecy and how such an understanding would have changed the disciples' expectation?

While on the road to Emmaus, Jesus was very harsh in His language to those two who were so disheartened and thought He could not have been the Messiah. What did He say to them?

Obviously, He hadn't taken a Dale Carnegie course on how to win friends and influence people. Had he been as positive as Robert Schuller and today's Christian psychologists, and formed a coalition with the rabbis (Evangelicals and Circumcisers Together—ECT?) as today's leading

evangelicals have done, He wouldn't even have gotten crucified and there would be no salvation!

Bluntly, Jesus said, *"Ye fools, and slow of heart to believe
all that the prophets have spoken. Ought not Christ to have
suffered these things and to enter in to his glory?"* Why
were they fools? Because they had not heeded all that the
prophets had spoken. The same is true of many evangelicals
today. Many do not study prophecy seriously and give it the
attention that it deserves.

The Coming Counterfeit Kingdom of Antichrist

Nor do the Jews of today have any better understanding of
prophecy than those in Jesus' day. They reject Jesus because
He didn't bring peace and establish the promised kingdom
on David's throne, and they are looking for a man who will
do that.

Indeed, Antichrist will establish a counterfeit of that
kingdom, and the world, including Israel, will follow him.
For good reason, Jesus said, *"I am come in my Father's
name, and ye receive me not: if another shall come in his
own name, him ye will receive"* (John 5:43).

Tragically, a lot of Christians are working to establish
that counterfeit kingdom. The Kingdom-Dominionist and
Reconstructionist thinks that the job of the church is to
establish peace, to clean up secular society, to oppose all the
evils out there, to turn America into a moral society and to
take over the world for Christ. That's not the commission
that Jesus gave His disciples, a commission which has been
passed on to us today.

Just as the disciples in Jesus' day were confused about
how and when the kingdom would be established, so there
is confusion on the same subject among Christians today.
We cannot emphasize too much the importance of understanding prophecy and taking it seriously.

In fact, the Bible gives the time frame in which the Messiah had to come. In Galatians 4:4 Paul writes, *"But when the fulness of time was come, God sent forth his Son."*

At the precise time that had been prophesied, God brought forth His Son. What time was that?

Well, we know that He had to be of the seed of David. That's why The New Testament begins with the genealogy of Jesus. He's not the Messiah unless He is of the seed of David. We have His genealogy in Matthew, where His lineage is traced through Joseph. He was not His father, but the head of the household through whom the kingly line must come.

Luke, however, traces the genealogy through Joseph's father-in-law, Mary's father. Most Bibles state that in the marginal note. Thus, through Mary and Joseph, on both sides, our Lord Jesus Christ is of the seed of David.

But, in A.D. 70, when Jerusalem, the Temple and the city were destroyed, the genealogical records were destroyed. It's too late for a Messiah to come along today and claim that he's of the household of David. He can't prove it now as the Bible proves it of Jesus.

So, we know, first of all, that the Messiah had to come when the genealogical records were there to prove his lineage.

The Messiah also had to come when the Temple was there. Malachi 3:1 refers to *"...the Lord, whom ye seek...."* He's the Messiah Israel was to expect. He's the Lord, but they didn't and still don't know that. He is God, that babe born in Bethlehem. A babe is born, a Son given, the eternal Son of God is given and *"...the government shall be upon his shoulder..."* (Isaiah 9:6). Thus, we know He's the Messiah. *"...his name shall be called Wonderful, Counsellor, The mighty God, The everlasting Father, The Prince of Peace."*

So when Jesus said, *"I and my Father are one,"* He meant one in *essence*. He is Yahweh; He is Jehovah; He is God. Thus, Malachi says, the Lord will suddenly come to His Temple. Therefore, the Temple had to be here. And Jesus came into the Temple suddenly, as prophesied, and threw out the moneychangers and he cleansed the Temple, as the Scriptures said He would: *" For the zeal of thine house hath eaten me up..."* (Psalm 69:9).

The Temple had to be there, the genealogical records had to be there, and the Temple and city of Jerusalem had to be destroyed shortly after His coming.

But there is more: In Genesis 49:10, in blessing his sons, Jacob said to Judah: *"The sceptre shall not depart from Judah, nor a lawgiver from between his feet, until Shiloh come; and unto him shall the gathering of the people be."* So if the people were going to follow Him, He must be the Messiah.

When did the sceptre depart from Judah? Historians tell us it was about A.D. 7. Israel was under the heel of Rome, but it still had a great deal of autonomy in the practice of religion, and to practice Judaism the Israelites had to be able to exact the death penalty, which was required for a breach of the Law. You picked up sticks on the Sabbath and you were stoned. You badmouthed your parents, and you were stoned. You committed adultery and you were stoned. In A.D. 7, the Jews lost that right.

In John 18, when the rabbis brought Jesus to Pilate, Pilate told them to take Him and judge Him according to *their* law. The rabbis said, "We can't. He deserves the death penalty according to our law, but it is not lawful for us to put any-one to death." They had lost that right and they acknowl-edged it. Not that they were sticklers for obeying Roman law — they tried to stone Jesus a number of times, and they stoned Stephen.

So there was a definite time frame within which the Messiah had to come. We know that the stipulated time frame is now past. What we await now is the return of Christ. No date for that is given. We are to expect Him at any moment.

Bible-believing Christians believe in the imminency of Christ's return. That is what The New Testament teaches. Consider these verses: *"...unto them that look for him shall he appear..."* (Hebrews 9:28).

"For our conversation is in heaven; from whence also we look for the Saviour..." (Philippians 3:20).

"...Ye turned to God from idols to serve the living and true God;

"And to wait for his Son from heaven" (1st Thessalonians 1:9–10).

"Looking for that blessed hope, and the glorious appearing of the great God and our Saviour Jesus Christ" (Titus 2:13). The early church expected Christ at any moment: They were watching and waiting for Him.

Two dear brothers met us at the airport one night because they knew when we were arriving. They weren't there a week or a month ahead, scanning the skies for our arrival.

The New Testament indicates that the Christians were watching for Jesus, and Jesus said in Luke 12:35–36,*"Let your loins be girded about, and your lights burning;*

"And ye yourselves like unto men that wait for their lord."

The Difference Between Rapture and Second Coming

The moment He comes you are ready for Him. The Bible surely teaches imminency in the expectation of the early church. No signs must precede the Rapture; nothing must occur before that great event can take place. The *signs* will signal the Second Coming to *Israel*, when Christ returns with His saints to rescue Israel in the midst of Armageddon—and those signs are already in the world all around us today.

From the Past, Just a Few Of the False Prophets and Their Prophecies

Many people have tried to set dates to establish the kingdom. You probably remember Maharishi Mahesh Yogi, founder of the Transcendental Meditation (TM) movement, who declared that 1979 was the first year of the Age of Enlightenment. We've been "enlightened" for the last 19 years, in case you didn't know that.

Do you remember that Herbert W. Armstrong predicted that his Worldwide Church of God would be raptured to the ancient city of Petra in 1972 and that Christ would return to the Earth in 1975?

In 1970, Elijah Muhammad, the founder of the Nation of Islam (succeeded by Farrakhan), prophesied to his Black Muslim followers that God's return to North America was imminent. It hasn't happened yet.

Mormonism boasts of its prophets. Joseph Smith declared in 1835 that Christ would return within 56 years. Well, if you know how to add, you know that's long past. Smith declared that many living then would not taste of death until Christ had come. That was another of his many false prophecies. It is amazing that evangelicals fall into some of the same ideas.

Charles Taze Russell's false prophecies formed the basis for what became known as the Watchtower Bible and Tract Society, the Jehovah's Witnesses of today. He declared that the Second Coming had taken place invisibly in 1874. Well, you can claim a lot of things if they're invisible! He said the Lord was truly present, and in 1914 the faithful (that's the 144,000) would be translated to heaven and the wicked would be destroyed and Armageddon completed.

In the early 1920s, the JWs zealously distributed, on the streets and door-to-door, their literature, "Millions Living Today Will Never Die." One of their favorite dates was 1925. You may remember they said that the patriarchs would return to this Earth at that time.

The Jehovah's Witnesses even built a house in San Diego which they tried to deed to King David. This was the house in which the patriarchs would live when they arrived in 1925.

Well, it didn't happen and they quietly sold "David's" house in 1954. They have given many false prophecies about the return of Christ. One of their books, published in the '40s, was called *Children*. It suggested that plans to marry and have children should be postponed until after Armageddon, which was imminent. They've had a long wait.

Seventh Day Adventism is based upon some of these false prophecies. William Miller made a number of predictions, but the final revised date for the return of Christ was October 22nd, 1844.

Ellen G. White, the prophetess for the Seventh Day Adventists, confirmed that date. When it did not happen visibly, she said Christ had *invisibly* returned—that He had entered the "inner sanctuary" of heaven.

Now, that's amazing, because Stephen saw Him at the right hand of God (Acts 7:55–56). I guess God wasn't in the inner sanctuary of heaven yet? And Jesus had been waiting in some outer court of heaven all these years?

On October 22, 1844, Christ supposedly went into the inner sanctuary to begin what Ellen G. White called the "investigative judgment." She blasphemously said that Christ's blood brought our sins into the sanctuary. Instead of cleansing us from sin as the Bible says, His blood brought our sins into the sanctuary in heaven and He began its cleansing, a work He's been doing ever since!

Let me give you a quote or two from Mrs. White (whose writings are regarded on the same level as Scripture by Adventists even today), showing that she taught salvation by works:

> Our acts, our words, even our most secret motives, all bear their weight in deciding our destiny. Though forgotten by us, they will bear their testimony that justify or condemn. When any have sins remaining upon the books of record unrepented of and unforgiven, their names will be blotted out of the Book of Life.
>
> Each one of you needs to be working with your might to redeem the failures of your past life. God has placed you in a world of suffering to prove you, to see if you will be found worthy of the gift of eternal life.

She speaks of the gift of eternal life, but you can't be worthy of a gift, can you? A gift must be accepted as a gift. You can't earn it. This teaching of the "investigative judgment" is one of the major heresies of the Adventists.

Here are a few of White's other false prophecies: that old Jerusalem would never be built up again; that she would be alive at the Rapture; that Christ would return before slavery was abolished; that the Adventists of her day would be alive at the Rapture, and so forth. Like so many others, Ellen G. White succumbed to the temptation of setting dates for which there is no Biblical basis.

Benny Hinn, A False Prophet

We have many false prophets today who are setting dates. Benny Hinn is one of them. On December 31, 1989, Hinn said the following:

> The Lord tells me that about [19]94 –[19]95, no later than that,
> God will destroy the homosexual community in America by
> fire.

It hasn't happened yet, and I doubt that it will happen until
the whole world comes under God's judgment. It only takes
one false prophecy to make one a false prophet, and we
could quote many other false prophecies given by Hinn.

Hinn can't even get his testimony straight. In the PTL
Family Devotional, he said, "I got saved in Israel in 1968."

But in a 1983 message in St. Louis, he said, "It was in
Canada that I was born-again, right after '68."

Yet in *Good Morning, Holy Spirit*, one of his books, he
says that he was converted in 1972 during his senior year of
high school. The problem is, he dropped out after the 11th
grade. So if he got saved during his senior year, he never
was saved!

False Logic in Dating the Return of Jesus

Today, some people use the Scripture, *"...the third day
I shall be perfected"* (Luke 13:32) to date the Rapture. They
believe it means that in the third millennium, Christ will
rule. Therefore, the Rapture must occur around the year
2000. In fact, when He spoke these words, Jesus was referring to His *resurrection.*

I hope you're not getting all hyped for the year 2000.
I believe we're headed for the greatest confusion and disil-
lusionment in history. If Christ has not taken us out of here
by then, I think very few people will believe in the Rapture
after that. Some of the Reconstructionists have already told
me about the scornful letters they're going to write to me
after that date.

"Why, if Christ hasn't come by the year 2000, and things
are getting better and better, then what's this teaching about

the Rapture?" [More about that in "The Confusion of Purpose," Chapter 3]

Let me give you several quotes of what some people are saying about the year 2000. Matthew Fox, New Age priest, says,

> In the United Nations plans are underway for the great global happening of the year 2000. The planet is alive with excitement, awaiting a global renaissance. This is the next big date that's coming up, as you know.

John Nesbitt, New Age author and guru to Newt Gingrich, says, "The year 2000 is the most compelling symbol of the future in our lifetime."

Pope John Paul II said,

> It's only three years until the great jubilee of the year 2000. The church and civil community of Rome are called to play an important role in this event. [Indeed, they will!] The common conviction is that it will put our city at the center of world attention, giving concrete expression to the name, Caput mundi [Latin term for capital of the world], which it is commonly called. In fact, preparing for the year 2000 has become, as it were, a hermeneutical key of my pontificate.

This is a most important date for the pope. Pat Robertson, commenting upon the pope, says,

> Pope John Paul II stands like a rock against all opposition in his clear enunciation of the foundation principles of the Christian faith.

On the contrary, the pope denies the foundation principles

of the Christian faith. Pope John Paul II prays to Mary, the key figure in Catholicism, for salvation. In his "Prayer for the Marian Year," he said, "Sustain us, O Virgin Mary, on our journey of faith and obtain for us the grace of eternal salvation."

It is blasphemy to ask of Mary the salvation which Christ has obtained by His death on the Cross and offers to us freely by His grace. In his 1996 tour of Latin America, the pope said:

> All those who have at some time prayed to the Most Holy Virgin, even though they may have strayed from the Catholic Church, conserve in their hearts an ember of faith which can be revived. The Virgin awaits them with maternal arms open wide.

The pope wears the scapular, which promises that those who die wearing it "shall not suffer eternal fire." He heads a church which claims that its sacraments are "essential to salvation." This is not Christianity but a deadly counterfeit, which Pat Robertson and other church leaders commend.

No wonder, then, that Pope John Paul II doesn't even know whether he will get to heaven. We quoted New York's Cardinal O'Connor from *The New York Times*:

> Church teaching is that I don't know at any given moment what my eternal future will be. I can hope, pray, do my very best—but I still don't know. Pope John Paul II doesn't know absolutely that he will go to heaven, nor does Mother Teresa of Calcutta....

The Catholic church denies the sufficiency of Christ's sacrifice on the Cross and teaches salvation through works and ritual—hence, the uncertainty.

Robert Schuller has said that the 2,000th birthday of Christ could mark the end of the "reactionary" age, as he calls the years following the Reformation. He says the Reformation shouldn't have happened.

In fact, Schuller declared that before he dared to build the Crystal Cathedral, he took an artist's conception of it to Rome to get the blessing of the pope. He said, "I wouldn't build it without the blessing of the Holy Father."

Schuller has said that "Christ's church will be born-again in the year 2000."

Robert Mueller, former Assistant Secretary General of the United Nations and now Chancellor of the University for Peace, says:

> We need a world or cosmic spirituality. I hope that religious leaders will get together and define before the end of this century the cosmic laws which are common to all faiths.
>
> We must hope also that the pope will come before the year 2000 to the United Nations, speak for all the religions and spiritualities on this planet and give the world a religious view of how the third millennium should be a spiritual millennium, which will see the integration and harmony of humanity with creation, with nature, with the planet, with the cosmos, and with eternity.

I don't know how many of you are familiar with the book, *The Star of 2000—Our Journey Toward Hope*, by Jay Gary. I think it's one of the most dangerous books to hit the Christian market in recent years. It promotes the very ecumenism and delusion that concerns us. According to Gary's book, some of the celebrations for Christ's 2000th birthday will involve reenacting the journey of the Magi.

You can get on camels and follow the route the wise men supposedly took following that star to find Jesus. And when you get to Jerusalem, they'll have a Magi planetarium, where you can see a simulation of the star you've been following. Gary talks about a "Jesus" who:

> ...belongs to people everywhere, no matter what their race or creed...the hope of revolutionaries and evolutionaries...the star of 2000...the greatest religious genius that ever lived...the outstanding personality of all times...one of the greatest teachers humanity has ever had...the most important and influential person that has ever lived...the most intriguing figure...the man of the millennium....

Gary continues:

> You don't even have to embrace the theological Jesus to find Him worthy of a momentous anniversary tribute.

He's talking about a generic "Jesus" who is not the Jesus of the Bible, one who can be praised by anyone and everyone. He says,

> In the year 2000, we will have the greatest street party the world has ever seen.

If his plans (and those of others) come to pass, the whole world will be hailing a generic Jesus in the greatest delusion of all time. This will not bring the world to faith in the Jesus of the Bible, the Savior of sinners, but will take them further away from Him.

One would think that Christian leaders would denounce Gary's book. Instead, many commend it. Here are some of those whose enthusiastic endorsements appear in the book:

Dr. Joe Aldrich; Dr. E. Brandt Gustavson, President, National Religious Broadcasters; Dr. Bill Bright, President, Campus Crusade for Christ; Dick Eastman; John Dawson; Paul Cedar, President of Evangelical Free Church of America; Paul Eshleman, head of the "Jesus Project"; and, of course, Father Tom Forrest, head of A.D. 2000 at the Vatican.

I think the confusion of dates will reach its climax in the year 2000. We need to get back to the Word of God, know what it says, know what we believe and why we believe it, and be in love with our Savior who came 1900 years ago and who, before He left for heaven, said, *"I will come again and receive you unto myself, that where I am, there ye may be also."*

That is the great hope of those who have come to know Him and to love Him. Let us serve Him and witness for Him until that glad day comes! ∎

CHAPTER FIVE

A Confusion Of Hope

—by Dave Hunt

Summary

Christian psychologists declare that the
Bible is not enough to deal with current
emotional or spiritual problems, but that
we must look to extra-Biblical sources for
supplemental guidance. Roman
Catholicism and numerous other cults
insist that the Bible is not complete or
sufficient, and that the new revelations
from their founders are the final word.
We also see how the Faith Movement has
used a twisted definition of a single word
to lead millions astray.

*F*or I am now ready to be offered, and the time of my
     departure is at hand" (2nd Timothy 4:6)

I remember debating Karl Keating, a bright young lawyer
who is the leading Roman Catholic apologist in the country.
I love the Word of God and just reading that verse reminds
me of that debate. We were debating whether the Bible is
sufficient.

The Meaning of Sufficiency
Catholicism insists that, in addition to the Bible, we must
also rely upon tradition as of equal authority and that only
the Roman Catholic Church can interpret Scripture.

Many evangelicals—though they affirm the *inerrancy* of
Scripture—also deny its *sufficiency*.

Christian psychologists, for example, declare that the
Bible is not enough to deal with current emotional or spiritual problems, but that we must look to extra-Biblical
sources for *supplemental* guidance.

I referred Karl to 2nd Timothy 3:16–17: *"All scripture is
given by inspiration of God, and is profitable for doctrine,
for reproof, for correction, for instruction in righteousness:*

*"That the man of God may be perfect, thoroughly fur-
nished unto all good works."*

These verses tell us that the Bible is all we need to be perfect—that is, mature and complete—and all that God
intends for us in this life, thoroughly equipped for every
good work.

**Catholicism's False Argument Against the Sufficiency
of Scripture**
Karl countered by referring to Cardinal Newman, a convert
from the Church of England to Catholicism in the last century. He said that Newman had pointed out that to take this

passage to mean that Scripture is all we need "proves too much," because all Timothy had was The Old Testament— and surely I wouldn't want to say that The Old Testament is all we need.

I told him that I was astonished that the Catholic Church could continue, for 100 years, to offer such an obviously invalid argument.

This was Paul's second epistle to Timothy, so he must have had the first in his possession as well and thus had at least two of Paul's epistles.

Moreover, in the next chapter Paul says, *"The time of my departure is at hand."* He was about to be martyred, so this had to be his last epistle, which meant that Timothy had all of Paul's epistles, or the major portion of The New Testament. The Book of Acts must also have been written, because it would be unthinkable that Luke would conclude the Book of Acts without mentioning the death of Paul, had that occurred. So, Timothy and the rest of the early church had that book also.

In addition, Luke begins the Book of Acts with these words: *"The former treatise have I made..."* referring to the Gospel of Luke, which therefore had already been written and also must have been available to Timothy.

The fact is that Timothy had all of The New Testament with the exception of those portions written by John. In any event, when the Bible refers to the Word of God, it means *all* of it, not what had been written to that time. To imagine otherwise would mean that statements about God's Word in the Psalms, for instance, could only be taken to refer to what had been written up to that time, which is ludicrous.

To accept Newman's (and Catholicism's) interpretation would undermine the entire Bible. When Jesus quoted to Satan in the wilderness, *"Man shall not live by bread alone, but by every word that proceedeth out of the mouth of God,"*

He obviously didn't mean only what God had said up to that point.

And when Jesus said in John 12, *"The words that I have spoken will judge him in that day,"* He surely didn't mean only the words that He had spoken to that point. When the Bible talks about God's Word or Scripture, it means all of it, whether the statement is made in The Old Testament, or in The New Testament.

"Faith" Versus "*The* Faith"
Let me assure you that the Bible defends itself. You cannot escape it! Paul goes on in the next chapter to state: *"I have fought a good fight, I have finished my course, I have kept the faith."* Note that he says, "*the* faith," not merely "faith."

Jude, in similar fashion, tells us to earnestly contend, not for "faith," but for "*the* faith." Paul warns that in the last days *"...some shall depart from the faith"* (1st Timothy 4:1). What is the difference between "faith" and "*the* faith"? There is a vast difference! People believe many things; there are many so-called "faiths"—by which we mean "religions." But "*the* faith" is something precise that we must believe to be saved and to live the Christian life.

False Assertions of "Faith" Teachers and the "Faith Movement"
Many church leaders call themselves "faith teachers" and promote what has become known as the "Faith Movement." They talk a lot about "faith," but they deny "*the* faith." To them, faith is some kind of *force* that you *aim* at God to get Him to do what you want. Literally.

Leaders in this movement such as Kenneth Hagin, Kenneth Copeland and others, pervert Hebrews 11:3. That verse reads, *"Through faith we understand that the worlds were framed by the Word of God."*

They claim that what it really says is, "We understand that it was through faith that God framed the worlds."

With a slight twist they have turned *faith* into a *force* that God used to create the worlds. And because you are "a little god" (so they teach), you can *speak* the creative word just as God does!

Benny Hinn and Paul Crouch have insisted upon this Satanic lie on Trinity Broadcasting Network. In a TBN newsletter, Paul Crouch wrote,

> If we are not 'little gods,' we will apologize to you in front of ten thousand times ten thousand before the Crystal Sea!

Well, man became a false god through believing Satan's lie in the Garden and if Paul Crouch insists upon being a "little god" instead of repenting of that ambition, then he will not even be in that scene in heaven to make his apology.

You wouldn't want to be a little god, would you? There's only one true God, and He says, *"...Is there a God beside me? yea, there is no God; I know not any"* (Isaiah 44:8). God says that He has searched everywhere and there is no other true God, though there are many false gods.

Satan, in his egomania, declared, *"...I will be like the most High"* (Isaiah 14:14). Of course, that's the impossible dream because there can clearly be only *one* most High! The best Satan could achieve was to be a little god, a false god, a counterfeit god, a rebellious creature seeking to usurp the position of God. And he passed that ambition on to Eve and through her to all of her descendants.

Satan's promise was not that she could become God but "as gods" (Genesis 3:5). In other words, she could join the company of false gods who followed Satan in his impossible dream, and as a consequence, would come under God's judgment for her rebellion.

There is only one true God, so Crouch, Hinn, Copeland and the others ought to recognize that in claiming to be "gods" they can only be "false gods."

Jeremiah 10:10–11 says it very clearly: *"But the LORD is the true God, he is the living God, and an everlasting king: at his wrath the earth shall tremble, and the nations shall not be able to abide his indignation.*

"Thus shall ye say unto them, The gods that have not made the heavens and the earth, even they shall perish from the earth, and from under these heavens."

So for Crouch, Hagin, Copeland, Hinn and the other "faith teachers" to claim to be "gods," while admitting that they did not create the heavens and the Earth, is to come under God's judgment and to perish!

"The faith" does not involve trying to get something from God. What is your goal? What is your hope? To be healed? To become wealthy?

I'm reminded of the newlyweds on their honeymoon. The young man began to have some second thoughts as to the genuineness of his bride's affection. Finally, he asked her, "Are you really sure that you didn't marry me just because my father left me a fortune?"

She replied, "Sweetheart, how could you think such a thought! I would have married you no matter who left you a fortune!"

"What's In It For Me?" Really?

In one of Oral Robert's books, he declares that we have the right to ask God, "What's in it for me?" The Bible calls that rebellion, robbing God of His glory. Jesus said, *"Whosoever will come after me, let him deny himself, and take up his cross, and follow me"* (Mark 8:34). Both Jesus and Paul set the example when they prayed to God, *"...not my will, but thine be done."* God alone must have all the glory.

Faith Has Moral Content

Moreover, *the* faith has moral content. It demands obedience; it changes our lives; it requires submission to God's will. Acts 6:7, for example, says, *"...a great company of the priests were obedient to the faith."*

Romans chapter 1 talks about the *"obedience to the faith"* and chapter 16 refers to *"the obedience of faith."* Paul tells Timothy, *"I have kept the faith."* And in order to do that he *"fought a good fight."* Finally, Paul says, *"I have finished my course"* (2nd Timothy 4:7).

God has a course for each of us; a life we are to live to His glory. The essence of it is to keep the faith and to earnestly contend for this faith which was once for all delivered to the saints. Each Christian has been called of God to fulfill a specific plan for his or her life—and God alone can enable us to do it through the power of His indwelling Holy Spirit and through Christ living His life in us.

Who Are Christ's "Successors"?

I have debated a number of the leading Roman Catholic apologists. They defend their church's teaching that the bishops and cardinals are the successors to the original apostles, and that the pope, of course, is the successor to Peter.

In discussing this with a dear Catholic lady, I said, "Well, if Peter was the first pope, he didn't get off to a very good start. If Peter (instead of Christ Himself, as the Bible teaches) is the rock upon which Christ built the church, it has a very unstable foundation."

Christ had no sooner said, *"...upon this rock I will build my church..."* than He gave Peter a stunning rebuke: *"...Get thee behind me, Satan..."* (Matthew 16:17–23).

The "first pope," if that's who Peter was, certainly wasn't *infallible* as Rome claims for its popes. The very first thing Peter did after allegedly being made pope was to deny that Christ must go to the Cross. When Jesus said that He *"must go unto Jerusalem...be killed, and be raised again the third day,"* Peter *"...began to rebuke him, saying, Be it far from thee, Lord; this shall not be unto thee."* Thus, Peter denied the very heart of Christianity. Not a good start for the "first pope"!

In the very next chapter, on the Mount of Transfiguration, when Jesus is talking with Moses and Elijah, Peter makes another serious denial of the faith involving Christ's deity. He lowers Christ to the level of the prophets when he says, *"Let us make here three tabernacles; one for thee, and one for Moses, and one for Elias"* (Matthew 17:4). And then, when Christ is being tried before the Sanhedrin, Peter denies Him with oaths and cursing (Matthew 26:74). Not a very auspicious beginning for the "first pope."

But back to the Roman Catholic claim that its bishops are the successors of the apostles. The truth is that all Christians are the successors to the apostles. The faith was delivered to the saints to defend it from contamination or compromise. If you are a Christian, you are a saint of God, sanctified and set apart to His work.

A saint is not some special person who did miracles and is voted in by the Congress of Cardinals long after his or her death, as Catholicism insists, but every Christian is a saint, and they have that status while alive on this Earth, not just in heaven.

The epistles were written to the Christians living in various cities and they were addressed as saints: the saints at Colossi, at Philippi, and Corinth, et cetera.

And how did those of us who are Christians today come into the faith which we are to live and defend? Well, somebody led *you* to Christ, did they not? And someone led *them* to Christ, and so forth back to the original disciples. When Jesus sent the original disciples forth, He said, *"Go ye into all the world and preach the gospel"* (Mark 16:15). He commissioned His disciples to make disciples and said they were to teach *"...them to observe all things whatsoever I have commanded you"* (Matthew 28:19–20).

In simple terms, then, the first disciples were to make disciples and they were to teach those disciples to obey everything Christ had commanded the original twelve. And that included that they (the new disciples) were themselves to make more disciples, and they in turn were to teach them to obey everything the Lord had commanded the original twelve—which, of course, included that they were themselves to make additional disciples and to teach them to observe everything Christ had commanded the original twelve, and so forth, generation of new disciples after generation of new disciples.

That command has finally come down to you and to me today. We have become the disciples of Jesus through those who were the disciples of the disciples of the disciples on back to the original twelve. So we, not the Roman Catholic bishops, are the true successors of the apostles!

God's Plan, Our Purpose
God has a wonderful plan and purpose for each of us as Christians, disciples of our Lord Jesus Christ. I often think of Paul's epistle to the Colossians. It ends, *"And say to Archippus, Take heed to the ministry which thou hast received in the Lord, that thou fulfil it"* (Colossians 4:17).

I sometimes think of Archippus dozing off until he was suddenly brought back to reality by that challenge calling him by name.

If the Lord should call out our names this evening, He would say to each of us, "Take heed to the ministry that you have received of me and be certain that you fulfill it!" God's call upon lives is not just to pastors or missionaries, but we *all* have been called to be saints here and now, sanctified and set apart for the work God has for us in this brief life He has given us to live as His servants and representatives.

As successors of the original apostles, we are commanded to obey everything Christ taught them.

Paul said, *"I have fought a good fight, I have finished my course, I have kept the faith."* And he told us to follow him as he followed Christ (1st Corinthians 11:1). There is a course for each of us. We are to keep the faith.

One reason I wrote the book, *In Defense of the Faith*, was because as I travel around the country and around the world, I find a great problem. Young people who have been raised in good Christian homes and in fine evangelical churches, upon getting into high school, university, or the business world, lose their "faith."

The problem is that they never had a solid foundation in the Word of God. They knew what they were *supposed* to believe, but never knew *why*; they never had sufficient *proof* to be fully convinced in their *own* hearts and minds and thereby to convince others.

I don't like to be critical, but I think that a lot of today's Sunday Schools fall short. As a little boy in Sunday School. I was taught the Word of God by dedicated teachers who knew God's Word and lived it. These teachers knew and loved the Lord, loved God's Word, studied it and taught us from its pages, not from standard material.

Today, Sunday School teachers generally use material which comes from a publisher who is more interested in making money than in presenting the unchanging truth of God's Word and in helping youth to stand true to God.

They have watered Christianity down so far that it hardly means anything. It's certainly not worth either living or dying for. It's mainly to entertain, not to offend; it's meant to be positive, and it presents little challenge to young people, little that really inspires them to go on for God. Too often, Sunday School lessons are taught by a teacher who is too busy to personally study the Word of God. Instead, he or she has a generic lesson from a publisher.

Many couldn't stand toe to toe with an atheist, a Buddhist, or a Hindu, and put them to flight. Consequently, many cannot pass on to their pupils a solid basis for standing firm for Christ in the face of the opposition, deception and temptations they are going to face.

I love to read the Book of Acts to see how the early church stood up to the opposition to the Gospel in its day.

Paul is a great inspiration and example. In Acts 9, immediately after his conversion, Paul confounds the Jews in Damascus, proving from the Scriptures that Jesus is the Son of God, that He is the promised Messiah. The Jews have two choices: either they will receive Christ, or they will kill Paul—and they opt for the latter.

Three years later (in that same chapter) we find Paul in Jerusalem confounding the Greeks, and they go about to kill him as well. One of my favorite verses is Acts 18:28. It is not about Paul, but Apollos: *"...he mightily convinced the Jews, and that publicly, shewing* [proving] *by the Scriptures that Jesus was Christ."*

If young people are taught the Scriptures and have that solid foundation in God's Word, they will not "lose their faith" when they get into high school or university, or be influenced by the media to go astray after this world. *If you lose your faith, you never had it.* We all need to know and understand, and then to stand upon the unshakable foundation of the Word of God. *"...I have kept the faith,"* said Paul. You can't shake me because I know the truth and I can prove it from the solid basis of the Word of God.

I love to go to universities and state (and I don't care how many Ph.D.s may be in the audience) "I will prove to you

that God exists. I will prove to you that the Bible is God's
Word. I will prove to you that Jesus Christ is the true and
only Savior of sinners. And I challenge anyone to refute it."
No one can refute God's Word, and if we know it thoroughly, we have a solid foundation to stand upon.

From A Christian Home To a Pagan Meditation Room
Phil Jackson, coach of the Chicago Bulls, is a tragic example of someone raised in a Christian home by parents who
pastored a church, yet he never understood Christianity and
therefore "lost" his faith at the university.

Apparently he didn't have the best of teaching, because
he seems to have equated Christianity with "speaking in
tongues." He tried unsuccessfully to get this thing called
"tongues," and when he failed, he gave up on Christ alto-
gether. This is clear from his autobiography, *Sacred Hoops*.

Having rejected a false Christianity, a caricature of the
truth, he turned to the occult, to Zen Buddhism and Native
American spirituality. It would break your heart that someone raised in a supposed Christian home could reject Christ
and turn to paganism, but this is happening to many today.
Jackson writes:

> The team room at the Sheri L. Berto Center is the perfect set-
> ting for an epiphany. It's the inner sanctum of the Chicago
> Bulls—a sacred space adorned with Native American totems
> and other symbolic objects I've collected over the years. On
> one wall hangs a wooden arrow with a tobacco pouch tied to
> it—the Lakota Sioux symbol of prayer [he's rejected prayer to
> the God of the Bible and to Jesus Christ] and on another, a bear
> claw necklace which, I'm told, conveys power and wisdom
> upon its beholder. [Incredibly, he has rejected Christ and now
> believes that a bear claw necklace zaps those who merely look
> at it with power and wisdom!]

The room also contains the middle feather of an owl (for
balance and harmony); a painting that tells the story of the
great mystical warrior, Crazy Horse, and photos of a white buffalo calf born in Wisconsin. To the Sioux, the white buffalo is
the most sacred of animals, a symbol of prosperity and good
fortune.

I had the room decorated this way to reinforce in the players' minds that our journey together each year, from the start
of training camp to the last whistle in the playoffs, is a sacred
quest. This is our holy sanctuary...where the spirit of the team
takes form.

What a tragedy! Here is a man raised as a boy in a supposedly Christian home. His parents were not just ordinary
Christians, but pastors of a church, yet he has rejected God
and Christ. He has rejected the Word of God and turned
instead to Native American myths about buffalo calves and
shamans turning into animals. He has embraced totems and
fetishes as the source of spiritual power.

And sadly, he has led most of his team (some of whom
were also raised in Christian homes) into the same delusions.

He tells how he led the team in Zen Buddhist meditation.
Michael Jordan, at first, just peered around to see if anyone
else was doing it, and then he began to "meditate" as well.
And now Jordan imagines that he is at times in touch with
the spirit of his murdered father.

Jackson quotes an Indian shaman to support his new
"faith":

> We are Earth people on a spiritual journey to the stars. Our
> quest is to look within, to know who we are, to see that we are
> connected to all things, that there is no separation but in the
> mind.

On the contrary, we are all separated from God by sin until we are reconciled through the death of Christ and our personal faith in Him as our Savior.

Without Christ, mankind is not on a journey to the stars (whatever Jackson may think that means) but on the way to an eternity separated from God in the *lake of fire*.

Jackson says that his mother hung John 3:16 on his wall, but he obviously didn't understand it.

He tells of trying to live a good enough life to be saved and that this is what John 3:16 means, when of course it teaches the opposite—that we are sinners for whom Christ died, not capable of living a good enough life to merit heaven.

Jackson has a confused hope. He has become a *pagan*, like recently deceased Carl Sagan, who worshipped the creation instead of the Creator.

I recently spent some time talking with the man sitting next to me on an airplane. He was a New Ager, and when we finally got down to truth and reality, we lost our communication, though he did say something that I don't think I'll easily forget.

He said that Carl Sagan was the only man with a big enough ego to star in a film about the Cosmos, which had to play second fiddle to him. Sagan would assume a seemingly reverent attitude in the presence of the Cosmos and declare,

> Just imagine! Some of the hydrogen atoms in my body were once part of a distant star system, and they will continue throughout the universe!

That's a pitiful hope. Somehow, I can't identify with the hydrogen atoms in my body. There's a vast difference between atoms and molecules and the soul and spirit of man. Hydrogen atoms know nothing of love or truth.

Paul says in 2nd Timothy 4:8, *"Henceforth there is laid up for me a crown of righteousness, which the Lord, the righteous judge shall give me at that day: and not to me only, but unto all them also that love his appearing."*

Do you love His appearing? I think that is the secret. Colossians 3 begins, *"If ye then be risen with Christ, seek those things which are above, where Christ sitteth on the right hand of God.*

"Set your affection on things above, not on things on the earth.

"For ye are dead, and your life is hid with Christ in God.

"When Christ, who is our life, shall appear, then shall ye also appear with him in glory.

"Mortify therefore your members which are upon the earth; fornication, uncleanness, inordinate affection, evil concupiscence, and covetousness, which is idolatry.

"Put on therefore, as the elect of God, holy and beloved, bowels of mercies, kindness, humbleness of mind, meekness, longsuffering" (Verses 1–5, 12).

Colossians 3 presents in the clearest language what the Christian life should not be, and then what it ought to be. In verses 5 and 12 the little word *"therefore"* refers, of course, to the verses that went before. What they present provides the reason for what follows.

On what basis can we mortify the evil in our bodies and put on the Christian graces which are the very life of Christ? It is because we are dead and our life is hidden with Christ in God. We cannot live the Christian life in our own strength. But Christ, who is our life, can live that life through us as we yield to Him by faith. Our great hope is that when He appears, we shall appear with Him in glory.

Paul is telling us in the clearest terms that the secret of victory in his life was that he loved Christ's appearing. He says the same to Timothy: *"Henceforth there is laid up for me a crown of righteousness, which the Lord, the righteous judge shall give to me in that day. And not to me only, but to them also that love his appearing"* (2nd Timothy 4:8).

If we love His appearing, we will have no love for the things of this world and will be delivered from Satan's wiles to live for our Lord. Our hope will not be to get what we want from God or to become little gods, but to honor Him and to be with Him in heaven praising and worshiping Him forever!

In contrast, for many Christians today the great hope is not for Christ to take them into His presence. They no longer believe in the Rapture. Their great hope is to take over the world and to hand it to Christ to rule over when He returns, not to take them to heaven, but to rule here upon Earth.

For others, the hope is to turn America into a Christian country so that it will be a safe place for their grandchildren.

For still others, the hope is to retire and enjoy some leisure years. They want to enjoy themselves and they have little thought of using the brief life God has given them to win others to Christ in order to present them to Him as trophies of His grace.

What Is the "Blessed Hope"?

Paul refers to the Rapture as *"...that blessed hope, and the glorious appearing of the great God and our Saviour Jesus Christ"* (Titus 2:13). Such a description would not fit if it occurred at the end of the Great Tribulation.

Let me describe the "Blessed Hope" of those who believe in a post-trib Rapture. They will refuse to take the mark of the Beast because to do so means to suffer the wrath of God and to be lost forever (Revelation 14:9–11). But without that mark they cannot buy or sell, so they will be eating out of garbage cans to survive. They will also refuse to worship the Beast or his image and as a consequence will be the targets of Antichrist's death squads. Death is the penalty for all who refuse to worship him.

So, folks, here is the "Blessed Hope" of the post-trib Rapture: If you can run fast enough to keep ahead of the world police, and if you can eat out of enough garbage cans to keep yourself alive, and if you survive the many plagues and horrors of the Great Tribulation—Blessed Hope, you'll be raptured at the last moment! That could hardly be the "Blessed Hope" to which Paul refers. It could not be called a "Blessed Hope" by anyone. Surely the "Blessed Hope" is the assurance that Christ could come at any moment and take us out of this world of evil and suffering.

Our great concern, however, is not to escape. We don't want to escape, but to be with our Lord. We are willing to suffer for His sake whatever is in God's will to His glory.

Paul reminds us that *"All they that will live godly in Christ Jesus shall suffer persecution"* (2nd Timothy 3:12). Christians are suffering persecution, imprisonment, torture and death all over the world today. It is estimated that more Christians have been martyred in this century than in all of the preceding centuries. The same could happen to us here in America if the Lord tarries much longer.

Our great longing is to be with our Lord. We are the bride and the Rapture will call us to heaven to be married to our Bridegroom, the Lord Jesus Christ who loved us so much that He took the judgment His own justice demanded for our sin.

Shouldn't the bride eagerly be looking forward to the wedding? If she isn't, it should be called off. We know for certain that our Bridegroom is eagerly looking forward to the wedding. How sad if His bride does not long to be with Him, but has set her affection so much on this world that she has forgotten her Lord!

Most of you probably remember the story of the preacher who asked all those in the congregation who wanted to go to heaven to raise their hands. Everyone raised his hand except one boy sitting in the front row. The preacher was concerned, so after the service had ended, he sat next to the boy and asked, "Son, don't you want to go to heaven?"

"Oh, yes sir," replied the boy. "I want to go to heaven."

"But I asked all those who wanted to go to heaven to raise their hands," said the worried pastor, "and you didn't raise your hand!"

The lad replied matter-of-factly, "Oh, but sir, I thought you meant right now."

Heaven is the place that everyone wants to go to eventually, but not right now. Are you ready to go now? Are you eager for your Lord to take you to His Father's house of many mansions? Or would the Rapture, if it occurred now, interrupt plans that you would rather see fulfilled here on Earth than be taken to heaven?

Turn to Luke 12:35–36, 40. Notice what Christ says: *"Let your loins be girded about, and your lights burning;*

"And ye yourselves like unto men that wait for their lord, when he will return from the wedding; that when he cometh and knocketh, they may open unto him immediately."

"Be ye therefore ready also: for the Son of man cometh at an hour when ye think not."

Christ not only urges a sense of imminency upon His disciples, but He reveals that the Rapture must take place before the Great Tribulation or the revelation of the Antichrist. Surely after those events, the hope and longing of every Christian, had the Rapture not taken place, would be for Christ to come and take them out of this world. Yet, He says He is coming when few, if any, will be expecting Him. That could not be at the end of the Great Tribulation!

The number 666 and the "Mark of the Beast"

- With the incredible pace of technological development, how will the actual global MARKING of people be implemented?

- What arguments, both legitimate and bogus, might Antichrist's officials put forward to CONVINCE the public to take the mark or number?

- How might the public be duped into believing the MARK is good?

Item# 2037 • Retail: $9.99 • 96 pages

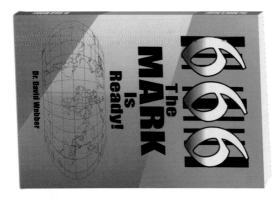

Dr. David Webber
The MARK Is Ready!

Let's imagine we are meeting in a cave in a wilderness somewhere and that we have been hiding in such places, moving from hideout to hideout during the seven years of the Great Tribulation.

We've managed to survive by eating out of garbage cans and have been able to keep one step ahead of the world police who are under orders to kill us. Some of the braver ones of our company have sneaked into towns now and then to peer into windows at night.

And there on CNN and other news programs, they have seen the very events taking place which the Bible prophesies for this period of time. They've seen pictures of the Jewish Temple rebuilt on the Temple Mount and viewed the restoration of animal sacrifices. They've seen the two witnesses of Revelation 11 preaching in the streets of Jerusalem; saw them killed by Antichrist; their dead bodies lay in Jerusalem's streets for 3 1/2 days and then, they suddenly were restored to life and taken up to heaven. Antichrist has erected his image in the Temple.

As each event occurred exactly as foretold in Revelation, we have marked its fulfillment in the margins of our Bibles with great excitement. We have marked the beginning of the 3 1/2 years and carefully counted the 1260 days.

Finally, the armies of the world have come against Israel, Jerusalem is surrounded and is about to go down in defeat with the extermination of the Jews. At that point we all yawn and go to sleep, saying in our stupor, "I don't think Christ would come now."

You say, "That's absurd." Of course it is. Then surely Christ could not have been referring to a post-trib Rapture when He said, *"At such an hour as ye think not, the Son of man cometh."* Jesus is saying, in fact, that He is coming at a time which, if we looked at the circumstances in the world, we'd say, "I don't think He will come now." That's exactly when He says He will come, when we wouldn't expect Him—and that can only be prior to the Great Tribulation and the appearance of Antichrist.

When is Christ coming? He said, *"As it was in the days of Noah...and Lot...."* Yes, those days were characterized by rampant homosexuality and much other evil, but that is not what Christ emphasizes when He elaborates upon what He means: *"They did eat, they drank, they married wives, they were given in marriage...they bought, they sold, they planted, they builded..."* (Luke 17:26–30).

It was a time of peace and prosperity, of feasting and pleasure. The last thing anyone expected was judgment. The contrast could not be greater in comparison to conditions at the end of the Great Tribulation. Nor could this be describing events even at the end of Revelation 6 when the Pre-Wrath Rapture is supposed to take place. Already at that time, the Earth has been devastated by war, famine, earthquakes and other incredible disasters—and Earth's inhabitants are crying to the rocks and mountains to hide them *"...from the wrath of the Lamb..."* (Revelation 6:16–17).

Matthew 24:29–31 says, *"Immediately after the tribulation of those days...he shall send his angels with a great sound of a trumpet, and they shall gather together his elect, from the four winds...."*

These verses have been used to teach a post-trib Rapture. This is not, however, the Rapture. The elect are the Jews who have seen Christ come from heaven to rescue them in the midst of Armageddon and who are being gathered together in Jerusalem from all over the world. It is not the Christians being caught up to meet the Lord Himself who has descended from heaven to meet them in the air, but angels are doing the gathering.

My father was from the old country, from England, and he used to tell some great old country stories. I remember one about a preacher who went by train to the north of England, where a certain lord had invited him to stay in his castle. Getting off the train, he was waiting at the station when he saw a cloud of dust made by an approaching carriage. Of course, he expected to see the lord's coachman driving. But as the carriage came closer, he was able to see through the dust, and astonished to see who was driving.

He exclaimed, "Why it's the lord himself coming for me!"

That's what we look forward to: *"...The Lord himself shall descend from heaven with a shout"* (1st Thessalonians 4:16) to catch up His bride for the wedding in His Father's house in heaven!

Critics say that the Rapture isn't even in the Bible. Rapture simply means an ecstatic catching away and I can't imagine a better description of such an event than this: *"...and the dead in Christ shall rise first: Then we which are alive and remain shall be caught up together with them in the clouds, to meet the Lord in the air, and so shall we ever be with the Lord"* (1st Thessalonians 4:16–17).

Christ said He was going away to prepare a place for us and that He would come again to receive us unto Himself (John 14:2–3). The only way He can catch us up to heaven to be with Him is through an event which could not have a better name than the Rapture!

I was talking with someone recently who said, "But supposing the Antichrist comes first?" I replied that such a scenario didn't fit with the Scriptures which have us watching, waiting and looking for Christ. If Antichrist had to come first, then we would be looking for him, not for Christ. "But suppose you're wrong and I'm right," this person persisted. "Think of the Christians who could be deceived. They don't think Antichrist is coming but they are expecting Christ as you have taught them. What a responsibility you have!

They could very well mistake this man of love and miracle power to be Christ! After all, you yourself say he will claim to be Christ."

"Deceived?" I replied. "On the contrary, we could not be deceived at all. The Antichrist comes to be the world ruler here on Earth. Christ comes to take us to heaven. The Antichrist can't catch us up to meet him in the air—and anyone who comes claiming to be Christ and doesn't Rapture us to heaven would be instantly recognized as a fraud! The very expectancy of the Rapture prevents the deception you imagine."

One of the major delusions in the church today, one which is growing rapidly, is a rejection of the Rapture. It is becoming far more popular to imagine that Christians are supposed to take over the world and that Christ cannot return until we do so. And then, when He returns, it will not be to take His bride to heaven, but to reign over the kingdom the church has supposedly established for Him here on Earth. One of the leaders in this movement to take over the world for Christ is CBN's Pat Robertson. He ran for the Republican nomination for president and failed to get it. Afterwards he was interviewed in *Charisma* magazine:

> If God called you to run, then why did you fail to get the Republican presidential nomination?

Pat's reply was astonishing:

> I suppose we could ask the same question of Jesus. God sent Him to be the Messiah of Israel; why did He fail the first time around and get crucified?

It was a failure for Jesus to be crucified? That Robertson could be so deceived as to make such a statement could well be the result of years spent in heeding false prophecies and in making them himself.

One of the most incredible false prophecies occurred in May, 1968, and was related by Robertson, who apparently did not realize how wrong it was. He wrote:

> It was dedication week of our new Portsmouth facility.... I'd just given a short talk on the bright future ahead of us at CBN, when all at once Harald Bredesen, our long-time Christian friend, came forward, placed his hand on my head, and began to speak a word of prophecy so powerful, I will never forget it as long as I live. For I knew God Himself was speaking to us that very moment. [God said], "I have chosen you to usher in the coming of My Son...." I was absolutely awestruck. God had assigned to CBN...to prepare the way for Jesus' Second Coming.

Robertson is not referring to the Rapture, but to the Second Coming of Christ to Earth to take the throne of His father David. I have the newsletters from that day in which Robertson used this false prophecy to raise huge sums of money, telling his faithful supporters,

> Wouldn't you like to contribute to the ministry that will usher in the coming of the Lord?

It seems that Robertson believes he is going to televise the Second Coming from his TV station in the Middle East. He doesn't seem to believe in the Rapture. He refers to a Tribulation period, but even during that time, he believes the church will be growing stronger in its takeover of the world.

If Robertson believes in the Rapture at all, it is a strange and mini event in which Christ catches us up to meet Him on His way down to Armageddon. We say, "Hi, Lord," and

continue with Him back to Earth in the midst of that greatest of wars. That's no way to treat one's bride. There's no
time for the Judgment Seat of Christ which we must all face,
no time for the marriage of the Bride to Christ, which takes
place in heaven.

Robertson began to receive revelations about the kingdom. He wrote a book in which he called it *The Secret
Kingdom* and claimed it operated under eight laws which, if
followed, would guarantee success in this world.

He stated that the unsaved and even occultists could use
these metaphysical laws, and he credited Napoleon Hill with
having utilized some of them in his occult system of success
taught to him by demons.

So, the kingdom which we will establish for Christ is to
be brought into being before His return by applying uni-
versal metaphysical principles. Writes Robertson:

> There can be peace, there can be plenty, there can be freedom.
> They will come the minute human beings accept the principles
> of the invisible world and begin to live by them in the visible....

By that he means all human beings, not just Christians.
What Robertson teaches in this and other books, such as
Beyond Reason, for example, is pure occultism. Following
Harald Bredesen's false prophecy, he writes:

> We know the King is coming and now it is our task to prepare
> the world's people to receive Him. Who could imagine a more
> breath-taking prospect? There is a great vision to fulfill, a great
> work to be done. This is why CBN must and will continue to
> strive to bring the good news of Jesus and of His Kingdom to
> renew this nation and this Earth. He's going to renew this
> nation and prepare [it] for Christ to come and rule over His
> Kingdom.

That is *a confusion of hope*! On the contrary, we are to preach the Gospel which saves lost souls and, instead of preparing them for Christ to return to this Earth, makes them citizens of heaven and prepares them to be taken to heaven at the Rapture of the church.

And here, we return to the problem which we referred to earlier, but didn't explain. If the real Jesus is going to catch us up and we're going to meet Him in the air, and you're looking forward to meeting a "Christ" with your feet on planet Earth, a "Christ" who hasn't come to take you to heaven, but to rule over the kingdom you've established for him on Earth, then you haven't been working for Christ. You've been serving Antichrist, who will indeed establish a kingdom here on Earth which Christ will destroy at His Second Coming.

Listen to Paul again:

"Henceforth, there is laid up for me a crown of righteousness which the Lord, the righteous judge, will give to me in that day; and not to me only, but unto all them also that love His appearing."

Is there anything that stands between you and the appearing of the Lord to catch up His bride to heaven? Is His coming your passion, or would it interfere with life as you have planned to live it here below?

I want to challenge each of us and especially my own heart. It's not too late to be victorious. It's not too late to have victory in Christ, to have that crown of righteousness awaiting us in glory, no matter what one's past failures may have been.

I want to challenge you that if we have this hope, not to change the world, (Christ said, *"I pray not for the world..."*) not to become wealthy, not to retire, but the hope of winning others so that they, too, can be with Him forever, there will be victory.

If we have a longing for His return and have set our affection on things above, not on things on the Earth, and we are seeking those things that are above, then we have the greatest motivation for successful, victorious, Biblical, Christian living and winning others for Christ.

I pray for myself and for each of us, that we will go away with that thought: *"Even so come, Lord Jesus!"* May that be the passion of our hearts. ■

CHAPTER SIX

A More Sure Word Of Prophecy

—by Alexander Seibel

Summary

An analysis of today's shallow doctrinal teaching shows how *easily* Christians are deceived. Seibel shows how Bible truth has been turned upside down in this process of deception. If believers acccpt Bible criticism even in a moderate way, they lose their spiritual defense mechanism and their discernment. What HIV does to the human body, erroneous liberal Bible criticism does to the church. Also, a leading "healing" evangelist's methods are exposed as those of a charlatan.

S econd Peter is an amazing epistle, whose basic theme is, "Despite growing apostasy, we can triumph as a servant of the Lord."

I'd like to sum up a few of my thoughts, beginning with chapter 2, where it says: *"But there were false prophets also among the people, even as there shall be false teachers among you, who privily shall bring in damnable heresies, even denying the Lord that bought them, and bring upon themselves swift destruction.*

"And many shall follow their pernicious ways; by reason of whom the way of truth shall be evil spoken of.

"And through covetousness shall they with feigned words make merchandise of you: whose judgment now of a long time lingereth not, and their damnation slumbereth not" (verse 1–3).

Bible "Criticism" and "Damnable Heresies"

Germany is a stronghold of Bible criticism, and there, in our present time, hardly anyone believes that 2nd Peter is a genuine epistle, written by Peter himself.

Those who consider the Bible to be inerrant are often described as "living fossils," and are generally thought to be somewhat behind the times. They're termed "fundamental," a word that can now unfortunately be used as a real battleaxe to crush any of their kind: It means, for some, "No fun, much damn, and a little bit mental (to say the least)."

I'm convinced that one of the reasons those in the school of liberal criticism of the Bible are so steadfast in labeling this epistle as false, is that it actually states the very things that are happening: *"...There shall be false teachers..."* among the people. These false teachers were prophesied to introduce *"...damnable heresies..."* that is, "destructive heresies." Now a heresy, or a cult, is usually destructive. Today, we've seen how this destructive element accelerates.

For example, consider the Aum cult in Japan, David Koresh and the Branch Davidians in Waco, Texas, and the Heaven's Gate group which committed suicide. All of these groups culminated in destruction as the result of these "false teachers" who denied, or slandered, the truth.

In Greek, the passage actually says they will "squeeze" (exploit) you out, and this is a typical characteristic of cults. Think of Scientology [a cult based on the writings of L. Ron Hubbard, now deceased] and others: they "squeeze" you out financially, and with feigned words.

The original text uses the Greek "plastos logos" (pl. plastoi logoi); more precisely, it uses the adjective form, "plastos," which means "formed or fabricated."

These false teachers base themselves on a fabricated world, with fabricated lives. We read much about this pseudo-world in Peter Lalonde's chapter on virtual reality [chapter two], and the takeover of fabrication.

The "Videotic" and "Idiotic" Society

As can you see, this is a time of fables; and our brother Peter Lalonde pointed out today's tremendous explosion of information and knowledge. Secular people complain that we have a new illiteracy—a "videotic," and finally an "idiotic" society. This is a result of the power of the picture, the medium which attracts our eyes.

In chapter twelve of this book, Peter Lalonde mentions "Star Trek" several times. More than twenty years ago, in the early seventies, I was asked to evangelize young people with the aid of a believing pastor during a confirmation camp in a state church.

We were led to observe that whether believers or not, these young people were under an influence, a demonic influence, which was not only affecting their mindset, but their psyche, and finally their whole being. We were slowly led to believe, after praying and counseling with them, that the cause was the TV series, "Star Trek."

This shocked me so much that I decided to never allow a TV in my house. I've never regretted this decision.

Later reports indicated that "Star Trek" creator Gene Rodenberry's main purpose for the series was to picture Satan as God and God as Satan.

Rodenberry was known to have counseled with spiritistic medium Phyllis Carmel, from whom he received ideas and themes for the episodes.

Other sources actually showed us that no other fictional TV show has reprogrammed the mind of Americans like "Star Trek."

The Fabricated Versus the Prophetic Word

Even an unbiased secular person called the "Mr. News" of our German state television claimed that television is a "decreed passivity, the execution of fantasy and the greatest time annihilator in the world." If our evangelicals in Germany and throughout the world would spend 10% of the time that they spend in front of the TV *on their knees in prayer*, there would be a glorious revival!

The very opposite of "logos plastos," this "fabricated word," is the prophetic Word. It is named so in 2nd Peter 1:19, *"We have also a more sure word of prophecy...,"* the "logos prophetikos."

This signifies that the Word will be fulfilled, either in grace if we obey, or in judgment if we disobey.

This doesn't mean that we can understand everything! The Bible is unfathomable, yet at the same time it is written so that a child can understand it.

For a brilliant mind, it is still fascinating, although it cannot always be immediately understood. Nevertheless, it means that if I'm ready to obey, it becomes true and alive.

So we've found the answer to the problem of the "plastoi logoi": it is the prophetic Word!

One of my first statements, that Germany is a stronghold of Bible criticism, needs to be explained. Many call themselves "evangelicals," and yet to them, the very idea of an inerrant Bible is ridiculous. The excuse they sometimes use is in Matthew 16:28: *"Verily I say unto you, There be some standing here, which shall not taste of death, till they see the Son of man coming in his kingdom."*

Our liberals say that Christ had a misconception about His Second Coming, and that He believed it would happen in His lifetime. Now, nearly 2,000 years have passed, and they claim that since He's not yet come, He must have been mistaken. If He's mistaken, then He's not the Son of God, and their conclusion is, as Paul writes: *"...we are of all men most miserable"* (1st Corinthians 15:19).

The Transfiguration

What's the answer to this liberal statement? It is what we read in all the synoptic Gospels [Matthew, Mark, Luke]. Right after our Lord makes this announcement in Matthew 16, in Mark 9:1 and in Luke 9:22, the transfiguration happens. The transfiguration was the Second Coming of Jesus in a *prophetic* setting. Had we lived in the time of Christ, we probably wouldn't have seen anything *outwardly* remarkable in Him, because he appeared like any other human.

The glory of God was veiled by (as it is stated in Hebrews) "the curtain of his flesh." However, there was one occasion when the Shekinah glory of our Lord shined through: on the Mount of Transfiguration. That's why John 1:14 can truthfully say that *"...we beheld his glory...."* They had been on the Mount of Transfiguration.

Also, Peter says (2nd Peter 1:16), as an eyewitness of His transfiguration: *"For we have not followed cunningly devised fables, when we made known unto you the power and coming of our Lord Jesus Christ....*" And here, the Greek word is "parousia," which is the technical term in the New Testament for the Second Coming of the Lord.

"*...But* [we] *were eyewitnesses of his majesty.*

"*For he received from God the Father honour and glory, when there came such a voice to him from the excellent glory, This is my beloved Son, in whom I am well pleased.*

"*And this voice which came from heaven we heard, when we were with him in the holy mount*" (2nd Peter 1:16–18). This is the exact description of the Mount of Transfiguration.

More Than One Coming

Peter, James and John were the first three human beings to realize that there were *two* comings of the Lord. This would have been a great mystery for anyone who, before the time of Jesus, had studied the prophetic Scriptures, because the Old Testament describes, on one hand, a suffering servant Messiah; and, on the other hand, a glorious conquering one.

No one could have understood that there were to be *two* comings. Some thought these contradictory prophecies would be fulfilled in two Messiahs, or perhaps one single person. In any case, it was a puzzle. This was the enigma we can now understand as believers of the New Testament.

On the Mount, we read that Peter asked: "*...Lord, it is good for us to be here: if thou wilt, let us make here three tabernacles; one for thee, and one for Moses, and one for Elias*" (Matthew 17:4).

Why does he suggest this? Because the Feast of Tabernacles was, on the one hand, a reminder of Israel's time in the desert; and, on the other hand, the symbol of the Millennium of Christ's rule. "*And it shall come to pass, that every one that is left of all the nations which came against Jerusalem shall even go up from year to year to worship the*

*King, the LORD of hosts, and to keep the feast of taberna-
cles"* (Zechariah 14:16).

Peter hadn't understood (How could he?) that there was
to be a time span of nearly 2000 years or more before the
"real" coming was to happen. He was convinced that it was
the "real" Second Coming, and not in the prophetic setting
as it was, so he suggested they observe the Feast of
Tabernacles.

From Matthew 16:16 to 17:9, salvation history is presented in a condensed form: Christ is, for the first time, publicly declared as the Messiah, *"...Thou art the Christ, the
Son of the living God"* (Matthew 16:16).

Later, the Lord predicts, for the first time, His future suffering and rejection (16:21). He then explains how we'll be
able to be saved (16:24 – 26). He continues to talk about his
Second Coming (16:27 – 28); and finally, He undergoes the
transfiguration (17:1 – 10), to give the disciples a prophetic
foretaste of His Second Coming.

Days In Which We Are Living: Sodom & Gomorrah
Continuing in 2nd Peter, the apostle describes the situation
of Lot and Noah (2nd Peter 2:5 – 7). By comparing our culture to this passage, we believe that we're now living in the
days of "Sodom and Gomorrah," when perversion is called
normal, and insiders call the 1990s "the decade of the homosexuals."

Because of this, we're now confronted with an increase
in the epidemic of AIDS. Perhaps equally threatening is
spiritual AIDS. What does this mean?

If believers accept Bible criticism even in a moderate
way, they lose their spiritual defense mechanism and their
discernment. Gradually, everything has to be tolerated.
What HIV does to the human body, erroneous liberal Bible
criticism does to the church.

"But chiefly them that walk after the flesh in the lust of uncleanness, and despise government. Presumptuous are they, selfwilled, they are not afraid to speak evil of dignities.

"Whereas angels, which are greater in power and might, bring not railing accusation against them before the Lord" (2nd Peter 2:10–11).

One aspect of this has been fulfilled in the cultural revolution of today. It began in the late sixties with the hippie era, and spread to Germany in the form of the student revolution in 1968. It was a rebellion against seen and unseen authorities.

"Spiritual Warfare" and "Prayer Walking"
Another fulfillment can be seen in the wave of spiritual warfare (mainly propagated by Peter Wagner) that originated in Argentina. One top figure, Carlos Anacondia, curses Satan, and uses all sorts of evil words against him. He is "bringing slanderous accusations" upon a being before the Lord!

Another form of "spiritual warfare" is the "prayer walk" program. Let me give you an example of this practice: Find a city, such as Los Angeles. Then find out which demons are responsible for this city (shown, for example, by visions), so that you have a specific insight into the spiritual (demonic) hierarchy. Then, organize a prayer walk in which people walk around the areas where the demons have been reported. This supposedly overcomes demonic forces. Congratulations. You've "conquered" a city for the Lord.

However, this is only a *spiritual fantasy*, spiritual virtual reality, and fits totally into the post-literal, "videotic" world of a generation that has grown up in front of T.V.

Our society is home to many illiterate citizens, with more and more graduates of our schools hardly able to read or write. Again, even secular people claim that TV has caused this degradation.

The "How" Of Spiritual Truth

Spiritual truth travels through the mind, not by feelings. Now, the Holy Spirit elicits feelings, but feelings don't cause the presence of the Holy Spirit. This can't be reversed.

The founder of a Bible school in Switzerland made a remarkable statement: "The Holy Spirit is the most glorious gift to the church when they obey, and the most dangerous one when they try to manipulate Him."

Talking of the last days (2nd Timothy 3:8), people are described as having depraved *minds*, not depraved *feelings*. Faith doesn't come by feelings, but by understanding: *"So then faith cometh by hearing, and hearing by the Word of God"* (Romans 10:17).

This picture is very powerful. The only way you can escape it is to close your eyes or run away. The Bible teaches us to *flee sin* and to *resist Satan*, not to *resist sin* and *flee Satan*. We must flee youthful lust, flee fornication, flee adultery. Now, when watching certain TV programs, many Christians don't flee. It pulls them in, with a seductive sequence, whether they like it or not.

"Scoffers Walking After Their Own Lusts..."

"This second epistle, beloved, I now write unto you; in both which I stir up your pure minds by way of remembrance:...

"Knowing this first, that there shall come in the last days scoffers, walking after their own lusts" (2nd Peter 3:1,3).

This is the self-love predicted in 2nd Timothy 3:2. This is an ego trip generation which scoffs at the Second Coming, saying *"...Where is the promise of his coming?..."* (2nd Peter 3:4).

In the time of the cultural revolution, students sold a book as Christians should sell the Bible. Written by a famous agnostic, Bertrand Russell, the title was *Why I Am Not a Christian.*

Because of all the heated argument about this book, as a young believer, I began to read it. The result was that my faith was strengthened. I read how Russell mocked people who believed in a literal Second Coming of the Lord. It's predicted that they're to do that!

In my situation as a new convert reading the Word of God, and seeing all this mockery and increasing attack against the Bible, I found the prophetic Word, written 2,000 years ago, a living and true Word!

"But the day of the Lord will come as a thief in the night; in the which the heavens shall pass away with a great noise, and the elements shall melt with fervent heat, the earth also and the works that are therein shall be burned up" (2nd Peter 3:10).

This statement really struck me because it has a direct scientific outlook.

Scientists, roughly two generations ago, mocked this verse because until the construction of the atomic bomb, it wasn't believed that an atom could be split; it could only change its physical state. In the Greek, "luo" means "to dissolve" (in fervent heat). This is exactly what happens when you explode an atomic bomb!

"Wherefore, beloved, seeing that ye look for such things, be diligent that ye may be found of him in peace, without spot, and blameless" (2nd Peter 3:14).

Peter mentions his "dear brother Paul," which wasn't an easy statement to make, because Paul had withstood him openly (Galatians 2:11). Peter could very humanly have had feelings of vengeance.

"As also in all his epistles, speaking in them of these things; in which are some things hard to be understood, which they that are unlearned and unstable wrest, as they do also the other scriptures, unto their own destruction" (2nd Peter 3:16).

The Distortion Of the Word

This was an illumination to me. Distortion of the Word is a leading characteristic of our days. Although the Bible has always been distorted by wicked opponents, it has never been warped in such a shameless and aggressive a way as today.

For example, regarding with the homosexual debate, liberals who claim to be "Christians" just brush the matter off, claiming that what Paul describes in Romans chapter one is irrelevant to the homosexuality of today.

I'm convinced of what the legendary Christian preacher Charles Spurgeon said: "There is nothing new in theology except that which is false."

The first female bishop of the Lutheran state church in Germany, Maria Jespen, was appointed a few years ago. When challenged with 1st Corinthians 14:34, that women should be silent in the church, she simply dismissed it as not being of Paul.

During a meeting in what is known as the "Toronto Blessing," a certain woman said: "The Bible says 'Be drunk with the Spirit.' A man stood up and answered; "My version says 'Be filled with the Spirit.'"

"Oh, but the Greek says 'to be drunk with the Spirit'" was the reply. This is false. The Greek uses the word "filled."

The Bible is twisted and distorted almost beyond recognition. If you don't know your Bible very well nowadays, you don't have a chance to survive these delusions and distortions. The suction of apostasy, godlessness, and seduction is too strong.

"Ye therefore, beloved, seeing ye know these things before..." (2nd Peter 3:17a). He declares we must know this; we must be well informed about the Word of God, *"...beware lest ye also, being led away with the error of the wicked, fall from your own stedfastness"* (2nd Peter 3:17b).

Notice that the word, "deception" comes up each time the epistles deal with the Second Coming of our Lord.

In *The Seduction Of Christianity*, which Dave Hunt wrote ten years ago, and for which he was very strongly attacked and criticized, we read that he was convinced that we are living in the last days. And this is because of an indication which many evangelicals have ignored or haven't had the discernment to detect: the Second Coming is always introduced with deception.

The Greek word for being "led away" has a particular significance: it means "to wander," "to be unsteady" (referred to again in Matthew 24:4 and a stronger word in 2nd Thessalonians 2:3).

This "not being carried away" has a spiritual implication also: It means that you must not get sucked into this mindset and this error. After a certain time has passed, things that were so alluring and deceptive at first will come to light as being false.

Benny Hinn's False "Signs and Wonders"

A preacher and traveling "healing" evangelist named Benny Hinn came to Basel, Switzerland in November of 1993. He told the audience to hold each other's hands, and he then claimed that he had the gift of imparting the Holy Spirit simply by *breathing* on them.

He then discreetly signaled to his attendants to turn up the loudspeakers to the maximum volume. Then he stepped up to the microphone and blew into it. There was such an explosion of sound that people shrank back; and since they were holding hands they were literally pulled down by each other. Some people even broke bones.

In a letter to the editor, one man asked: "What kind of Spirit is this which allegedly is going to heal everyone, but first breaks their bones?"

In 1st Corinthians 12, Paul, when discussing the gifts, shows how to distinguish between the real and the counterfeit. This is what I point out in my book, *The Church Subtly Deceived*, which reminds us of 1st Corinthians 12:2, where it says *"...Ye know that ye were Gentiles, carried away unto these dumb idols, even as ye were led."* The active voice of this word, in the Greek, signifies "to be arrested."

For example, when our Lord was in Gethsemane, the soldiers came and "arrested" him. Here, the same word is used, but in the passive form which literally means, "to be torn away." This form of the Greek word perhaps most accurately describes the phenomenon of being "slain in the spirit," or losing self-control. This is what Benny Hinn is so proud of, and what Paul denounces as *false*.

It occurred to me as I was reading the Greek that when Paul explains the spiritual armor to the Ephesians, (chapter 6), the word "stand" is used three times. *"...that ye may be able to stand against the wiles of the devil"* (verse 11), and again in verse 13 and 14. In "faith healer" meetings, people aren't standing, they're *falling*. Paul meant it to be primarily metaphorical, but here we have a literal fulfillment!

Later, the organizers of Hinn's debacle apologized for the fact that Benny Hinn had been a deceiver, and complained that they hadn't been warned about him.

Overcoming Falsehood and Error
"But grow in grace, and in the knowledge of our Lord and Saviour Jesus Christ. To him be glory both now and for ever. Amen" (2nd Peter 3:18).

This is the key verse of 2nd Peter, because it shows us how we are to overcome despite growing apostasy. In the first chapter he shows us how we have grace and peace through Jesus Christ, and here at the end, he uses the imperative: "Grow!"

This makes it plain to us that the grace of God is sufficient, not using fabricated words, but *the* prophetic and living Word.

This is my wish also, for you and for myself, that we should grow in the grace and knowledge of our Lord and Savior Jesus Christ! ■

CHAPTER SEVEN

Overcoming Last Days Attacks On the Family

—by Moody Adams

Summary

A seemingly endless parade of statistics indicates that families are deteriorating. Instead of a supportive, loving environment, the home has often become a battleground, even a killing field. Perhaps most significant about the fall of the family is that it was prophesied in the Bible as a sign of the endtimes.

Y ou don't have to go to Israel to see prophecy being
     fulfilled. Ancient Bible prophecies are racing to ful-
     fillment in America's homes. The Bible plainly laid
out a startling, unimaginable course for families in the last
days.

Those who are serious about building a winning family
understand what the family must face and how to overcome
in the midst of these circumstances.

Angry Satanic Attacks
In the unveiling of last-days events, the Bible says mankind
will come under greater Satanic attacks than ever before:
*"...Woe to the inhabiters of the Earth and of the sea! for the
devil is come down unto you, having great wrath, because
he knoweth that he hath but a short time"* (Revelation
12:12). Satan came down the first time with great deception,
but the Bible says he'll come down a second time with great
wrath, motivated by the fact he only has a short time. Men
will have to deal with an angry Devil who is in a great hurry.

A Man's Family Will Become His Foe
The Scripture says much of the Devil's last-days attack will
be directed against the family. Jesus foretold, *"And a man's
foes shall be they of his own household"* (Matthew
10:21,36). These were strange words in the first century,
when family members fought for each other. They were
close and devoted. Few then could imagine turning against
their own family. Yet today, some of the meanest wars
fought in America are waged inside the home!

The Love Of Many Will Wax Cold
When Christ was asked about the signs of history's last
days, He made the strange prediction that, *"...the love of
many shall wax cold"* (Matthew 24:12). In the day in which

He spoke, love was assumed to be a lifetime commitment. But in our generation, love refers to a passion that can cool as fast as an Alaskan summer.

A Fiercely Independent Feminism
In a day when there was no way a woman could be self-supporting, the Bible foretold that those circumstances would change.

A day would come, the Bible said, when women would no longer be dependent on men. It said they would become financially independent. Marriage would be little more than a way for a woman to take away her reproach:

"And in that day seven women shall take hold of one man, saying, We will eat our own bread, and wear our own apparel: only let us be called by thy name, to take away our reproach" (Isaiah 4:1).

Sadly, in the United States and across the world, this startling prediction is coming true.

Massive Murder by Family Members
In a far more horrid and amazing prediction, Jesus said, *"And the brother shall deliver up the brother to death, and the father the child; and the children shall rise up against their parents, and cause them to be put to death"* (Matthew 10:21).

When Christ uttered this prophecy, most would die to protect family members.

Today, more babies are killed by parents in America than by automobile accidents. At least 2,000 children under four years of age die every year from parental abuse and neglect and 18,000 others are permanently disabled.

A federal panel reported that violence directed at very young children has become a public health crisis. Advisory board chairman Deon Durby said:

> Since our study began in 1992, some 5,000 children have
> died at the hands of the very adults they depended on for
> safety and love.

The tragedy is not only that babies are being killed, it's also that society shows its approval by creating excuses for the murderers.

Susan Smith drowned her two children and explained the reason was that she had been sexually abused when she was a young girl.

In North Carolina, Douglas Monts shot his three little children to death.

After he shot them in the head, he set his van on fire and then killed himself.

Police Chief James Braley shifted the blame from the killer by saying, "Society has failed to prevent this kind of thing from happening."

Donna Jean Flemming, 23, threw her two young sons from an overpass into the mouth of the Los Angeles River on February 21, 1997 and jumped in after them. The youngest boy drowned.

Detective Bill MacMillan explained, "She was a little depressed."

Tildon Harris, a 26-year-old successful young business-man in Baton Rouge, Louisiana, hired a man to kill his wife. After driving his wife to the Tinsel Town Theater on a Sunday, he parked the truck and told her he was going to get tickets.

The hired killer thought there was some mistake when he saw his hit was a woman. He caught up with Harris and said, "That's a woman!"

Harris replied, "Yes, I know."

The hit man said, "You want me to kill a woman?"

Harris said, "Yes."

The hit man went back to the car and blew the wife's brains out. Harris and the hit man were caught, and at the time of this writing, were awaiting trial for murder.

Statistics show that 20% of all murders in America are now family-related, making the home the number one danger zone.

In fact, many wives may have misplaced fears: FBI statistics show that the number one place American women get murdered isn't in some dark alley late at night, it's in their own bedrooms! And most American men are murdered in the kitchen.

Massive murders by family members is a startling new development. It is the very thing the Bible prophesied.

An Array Of Sins Will Devastate the Family
In Second Timothy 3:1–6, the Bible tells us:
"This know also, that in the last days perilous times shall come.

"For men shall be lovers of their own selves, covetous, boasters, proud, blasphemers, disobedient to parents, unthankful, unholy,

"Without natural affection, trucebreakers, false accusers, incontinent, fierce, despisers of those that are good,

"Traitors, heady, highminded, lovers of pleasures more than lovers of God;

"Having a form of godliness, but denying the power thereof: from such turn away."

The Bible predicted that these evils, which have plagued man from the beginning of history, would soar to such epidemic proportions that they would be a clear sign of the last days. Demonic lusts would ravage men's hearts, creating perilous times for society and devastating the family.

This is a prediction of sudden and dramatic increase in family violence, and that's exactly what we're seeing today.

Margaret Thatcher warned a Nashville audience about these
changes when she said:

> If you were born before 1945, you were born in the world
> where there was no T.V., no penicillin, no contact lens. A
> chip was a piece of wood, grass was something you mowed
> instead of something you smoked and Coke was a soft drink.
> A pot was something you cooked in and rock music was
> grandmother's lullabies.
>
> The illegitimacy rate was 3%. You know, they tell us the
> reason people fornicate and have illegitimate children is
> poverty. Well, during the Great Depression, it was 3%. Last
> year, in the most affluent society the world has every known,
> it soared to 31% of all babies born in the United States of
> America. The dangers of illegitimacy are there. They're
> more likely to drop out of school, use drugs, have emotional
> problems, commit violence, become criminals and produce
> illegitimate children themselves.

These are the kinds of things undermining the family.

Family Love Replaced By Self Love
The prophecy in Second Timothy says men are going to be
"...lovers of their own selves..." (2nd Timothy 3:2). The
Devil is motivating more people than ever before to foster
a passionate love for... *themselves.* He's convincing men
and women that they're justified in "looking out for number
one."

If you dig down to the very root of our disastrous family
problems, you find two people living together, pretending to
love each other, while they're carrying on a secret love
affair with... *themselves.*

After they cloned the first sheep in Scotland, one man
declared that he's having himself cloned. Then, with genetic

manipulation, he plans to have his clone's gender changed to female. When she grows up, he'll marry her. He explained, "The reason for doing this is I've never been able to find a woman that loved me as much as I love myself." Of course this was a joke, but Shakespeare said, "Many a truth is spoken in jest."

When a self-loving husband walks into the room while his wife is watching her favorite program on TV, he asks, "What else is on TV?" A good friend of mine solved the problem by buying two TVs. He put one on top of the other, and he ran a cord to his ear. This is a fantastic idea.

In New Orleans, Louisiana, a man took a different approach. He walked in the living room one night and found his wife watching her favorite TV program. He switched the TV to a ballgame he preferred. Without saying a word, she got up, went in the bedroom, got a shotgun and blew his brains out! These kinds of problems are rooted in self-love. "Don't mess with the T.V. when I'm watching what I want to watch!"

Ann Landers has perhaps given more marital advice to more people on more subjects than anyone who ever lived, despite having her own marriage fail after 28 years.

In one of her columns, she answered a woman who was trying to decide whether to stay married or get a divorce. Landers told her, "You know what I always say: Stop and ask yourself, 'Am I better off in this relationship or out of it?'" *That's exactly what a self-loving generation wants to hear.* Never ask yourself if the children are better off, or if the mate is better off with you staying in the marriage. Just ask yourself if you are better off.

Dr. Dean Edell is the host of a nationwide radio show dealing with medical topics. In his May 23rd, 1996 program, he got very upset, in contrast to his usually mild-mannered demeanor.

He told of a lady who had a baby born with a lung problem. When she was discharged from the hospital, she was told by the doctors that she'd have to keep this child in a very protective environment. Any irritants to the baby's lungs could be fatal.

"For instance," her doctor warned, "You can never let your child be around cigarette smoke. It could kill him."

She replied, "I smoke."

He said, "You'll have to give that up."

She quickly responded, "I'm not even thinking about giving it up. I'll give up the baby."

She put him up for adoption.

This is exactly what the Bible said would happen in the last days: men (and women) would be lovers of their own selves, and this self-love is devastating the home.

Covetousness Will Corrupt the Home

The prophecy says, *"...men shall be...covetous...."* Experts tell us the number one cause of divorce in America is money problems. One might think that, as rich as we are, we would be content. We are not. The Devil is stirring up a passionate love for more and more material things. We call it a "shopping addiction." God calls it "covetousness." It's wanting more than you can afford, wanting everything advertised on T.V., wanting everything the neighbors have, and wanting it right now.

It isn't that our generation has too little money; it's that we want too much. We want it *all*, and we want it *right now*. And we'll take it any way we can get it, even if it means family members have to *hurry up and die* so we can grab the inheritance.

One Cajun said his grandson asked, "Paw Paw, can you speak frog?"

He said, "No boy, I can't speak no frog."

The next day his grandson repeated, "Paw Paw, can you speak frog yet?"

Again he replied, "No boy, I don't speak no frog. Why do you ask such a dumb question?"

He answered, "Because mama said as soon as you croak, we're going to Disney World."

The average American family is living in more house than they can afford, driving more car than they can afford, wearing fancier clothes than they can afford and taking more vacation than they can afford.

Over a million American families are going bankrupt every year. Stop and think about it: This is the richest, most affluent society in the history of the world and we're setting records for... *bankruptcy*. Why? It isn't because we don't have enough money. It's because we covet more than we can afford.

The average American family is $6,000 in debt on their credit cards alone, not counting car payments and house payments.

Credit-card spending is a lot like sinning: You can have a whole lot of fun until the payment comes due. And when the payment comes due and the money runs out, the family starts the blame game, "You didn't have to buy that boat"; "You've got more shoes than Imelda Marcos"; "You spent a fortune on that hunting trip"; "You certainly didn't have to have a new dress." The relationship begins to deteriorate. Soon the family is finished.

Arrogant Pride
This last-days prophecy says, *"...men shall be... boasters, proud...."* You know what proud men are. They're the fellows who come home from work every evening and the first thing they do is ascend to their throne, sit down, bellow out orders and play God.

Proud men don't want to go to church, humble themselves and recognize that God is greater than they are. They
pay a big price for their pride. The average Christian family in America which attends church has an income of
$37,000 a year. The average family in America which does-
n't go to church brings in $23,000 a year. That means faith-
ful church members are getting paid $1,200 a month just to
go to church! But still, proud people don't need God.

Proud people are very competitive. They constantly seek
to elevate themselves above others. C.S. Lewis said, "Pride
gets no pleasure out of having something, only out of having more of it than others."

Proud people aren't concerned with whether their income
meets their needs. They're concerned with whether their
income is higher than their neighbor's.

They constantly compare their income, appearance, hair,
clothing, car, home, physique, and bank account to others.

Microsoft Chairman Bill Gates goes to work every morning at 6 a.m. The richest man in the world seems scared to
death that someone will pass him!

Pride is a spiritual cancer. It eats up the very possibility
of love or contentment or even common sense. Pride, when
it is full grown, leads to hate, envy, divorce and even war.

When I was a young preacher, I presented a sermon on
the Psalms that says, *"Be ye not as...the mule"* (Psalm
32:9). I titled it "Mule-headed Church Members." Before I
preached the message, I'd have the congregation sing, "I
Shall Not Be Moved"— their theme song. The last time I
preached that sermon, a man came up to me and said, "I did-
n't like your sermon." I said, "I'm sorry."

He explained he didn't like any mention of a mule. He
said when he was a boy, his daddy would give him work to
do. The mule wouldn't do the work, but he, the boy, would
get the whipping.

One night, his daddy told him, "Now son, first thing in the morning, you get out there, hitch up the mule, get all the merchandise loaded in the wagon and get it downtown."

The boy said, "But daddy, that mule...."

Daddy interrupted and said, "I don't want to hear about it. Just get the merchandise to town."

The man told me, "I went out there the next morning with a holy resolve that I wasn't taking another whipping for that stubborn mule. And I got all the merchandise loaded up, hitched the wagon up, and I optimistically shook the reins."

The mule just stood there. If you ever owned a mule, you know a mule has a spiritual problem. He's proud; nobody will tell him what to do.

The man told me, "I reached back and took the whip and tried to split that mule's back. He didn't budge. I got down and got me about a 12–foot limb and whipped that mule until it was two feet long and my arms were too weary to lift it. The mule never budged. I said, 'Well mule, I've got bad news for you.' I trotted up to the house, got an arm load of kindling wood, five gallons of kerosene and a box of matches. I piled the wood under his stomach, poured the whole five gallons on it and threw the match. Believe me, when the fire hit that mule, he moved—ten feet—and burned up the wagon."

There are people just that proud. They say, "I don't care if my children go to the Devil. I don't care if my marriage goes to divorce court. I don't care if my family goes up in smoke. I don't care. I have to have my way."

This is the arrogance that is ripping homes apart.

Disobedient Children

Then, the prophecy says we'll be plagued with disobedient, unthankful children. I have a fact that I can't explain. I bring it up not knowing what to say about it, but I learned a very

strange thing. A survey of prisons in Florida found that, out
of 40,000 inmates, only 13 were Jews.

In Texas prisons, a survey found that only two-tenths of
one percent of inmates were Jews.

A study in the military found there were only three Jews
out of 36,000 soldiers in the brig.

An F.B.I. man in Savannah, Georgia, heard me quote
these figures and went out and checked their computer.
They didn't have a single Jew in jail in that section of
Georgia.

Why? It could be that while we're a lot closer to the Bible
in the way of salvation, the Jews are a lot closer to the Bible
when it comes to raising children.

I've learned that a devoted Jewish father practices three
things every time his son comes into the room: No matter
how busy he is, he stops, gets up, kisses his son on the
cheek, hugs him, and says, "My son, I love you, you are
very important to me."

Evangelist and Christian apologist Josh McDowell has
often said that "rules without a relationship leads to rebellion."

Many people say to their pastor, "Preacher, I don't know
what's wrong with my kid. I've taught him right from
wrong."

Sure, dad gave him all the rules, but, what about the *relationship?* One survey showed the average American father
spends about two minutes a day talking with his child.

Parents are neglecting to love and discipline their children and the children are growing up disobedient and
unthankful.

Beverly Soberland attended my seminar on "How to
Raise Children Without Frustration."

She said, "I had a 15-year-old boy that was driving me
crazy. He was the most arrogant, insolent, rude kid. He just

cut me down all the time. I'd look at him, cry and think, 'I brought him into the world, I can't believe he's standing here talking to me like this.'"

After the seminar, a letter came to our office, in which Mrs. Soberland wrote, "It worked!"

The first time her boy said something smart, she marched him out on the front porch without a jacket in 24 degree weather.

He turned a little blue, got mad, and hit the door buzzer. She smiled and said, "Every time you hit the buzzer, I'm adding 5 minutes on the timer." She said he nearly froze to death, but he stopped his smart talk.

Fifteen-year-old Tommy Sullivan wrote a note that said,

> To the greatest demons of hell, I, Tommy Sullivan, would like to make solemn exchange with you. If you give me the most extreme of all magical powers, I will promise to kill many Christians.
>
> I promise to commit suicide. I will tempt teenagers on Earth to have sex, have incest, do drugs, worship you. I believe that evil will once again rise and conquer the love of God.

Tommy Sullivan went into the kitchen of his fine home one winter night, took a kitchen knife and stabbed his mother to death. He cut her hands nearly off. As she was trying to get away, he followed her through the house, stabbing her over and over and over.

The authorities found him the next morning in a snow bank near the house. He had cut his wrist, fulfilling his promise to Satan. He left the note by his body.

Satan is after our children. He's frantically working to turn them into disobedient, unthankful rebels so they'll self-destruct.

Sexual Perversion

Second Timothy gives another sign of the last days: *"...men shall be ... without natural affection."* Sex is the dynamite force God put in the human body to make a man, *"...leave father and mother, and shall cleave to his wife: and they twain shall be one flesh"* (Matthew 19:5). Jesus said it was designed to be the cohesive force that holds a man and wife together and keeps them together as they raise their children. Any time the sexual force breaks outside the confines of the married relationship, the family is undermined.

Vice President Albert Gore welcomed 150 gay and lesbian to his home and told them,

> Its a wonderful thing to do what you are doing, and that is devoting your life to others, this dedication is an outgrowth of the way you live your entire lives.

Well, here are some facts about the way they "live their lives." The Family Research Council in Washington, D.C. did a study which showed the life expectancy of a male homosexual is about 42 years. The life expectancy of a lesbian is about 47 years. Homosexuals have a much higher suicide rate, a higher automobile accident rate, and far higher disease rates. The way they "live their lives" is filthy and disease-ridden—it is killing them. And it is undermining the American family. A British author said, "The United States has turned into a sexual nuthouse."

This is what the Bible predicted!

Truce Breakers

The Bible said that, in the last days, men would be "truce breakers." One of the definitions of the Greek word used here is "A man is so dishonorable that he breaks the terms of the agreement he has made" (William Barclay).

When men promise to love until "death do us part" and then run out on their wives, they are breaking their vow. About 50% of American first marriages, 60% of second marriages and 70% of third marriages are ending in divorce. This breakdown of marriages exploded in the 1960s. This change reflects Bible prophecy. It is caused by people not keeping their vows.

In 1997, the State of Louisiana offered couples an alternative marriage. Called a "covenant marriage," it cannot be terminated without proving in court that the spouse has been guilty of adultery, abuse or abandonment.

At the end of the first year, only a couple of dozen couples had chosen the "covenant marriage."

Many have no intention of keeping their wedding vows if they're inconvenienced by them at all. They'll leave when and if they please, in the circumstances they decide.

While conventional wisdom says economic and industrial changes have broken up the home, David Blankenhorn wrote a startling book, titled *Fatherless America*, which says the real reason is:

> ...the shift toward expressive individualism, the idea that your basic responsibility is to yourself, which means that your obligation to others becomes weaker.

That obligation can become so weak that men and women don't hesitate to break their vow and leave. Blankenhorn says that's at the tap root of it all.

Self-centered parents break their vows with little concern about the horrible effect it has on their children.

A 25–year study by Walstein and Lewis, psychology professors in San Francisco, showed that half of the children from broken homes became seriously involved with drugs or alcohol. Half of these children end up with less education than their parents. Teenage girls with a father get pregnant 50% less often than their fatherless counterparts. Children living without a father are far more likely to drop out of school. Blankenhorn said that, more than any other factor, a biological father's presence in the family will determine a child's success and happiness:

> More than his being rich or poor, white or black, the children of divorce, and those born outside marriage, struggle through life at a measurable disadvantage.

Rampant Lust

The last-days prophecy says *"...men shall be ... incontinent."* This means they can't control their passions. Their lusts reduce them to mere slaves. Slavery to pornography, adultery, drugs, alcohol, hatred, unforgiveness and greed is making it impossible for many to succeed at building a home.

A young minister who won the "Preacher of the Year Award" at Liberty University, which produces many outstanding preachers in America, talked with me about his struggle with pornography.

He told me he had gone to a psychiatric hospital to try to get help, but he couldn't shake it.

Three months later, he got up one Saturday morning, went into his carport, sat down and blew his brains out.

A trail of lust ended with a young man dead, and a wife and two children devastated!

I discussed the case with a psychiatrist who said,

> Let me tell you something, pornography is an epidemic in America. We're now treating a huge number of college students that can no longer function sexually unless they first watch a porn film.

What type of husbands and wives will they make?

What Can We Do?

The same Biblical revelation that told us of the attacks of an angry Devil, tells us how we can overcome them and build successful lives and families. *"And they overcame him* (the Devil) *by the blood of the Lamb, and by the word of their testimony..."* (Revelation 12:11).

When Christ died on the cross, He not only paid for our sins, He also defeated our enemy. He bruised the Devil's head. He spoiled evil "principalities and powers." Through the blood of that cross, Jesus triumphed over our enemy!

We become partakers of this victory "through the word of our testimony."

Resist the Devil and testify in faith, "You won't enslave me with this lust. You won't make me neglect the discipline of my children. You won't pump me up with pride. You won't make me spend myself into hopeless debt. You won't break up my family. You've been defeated at the cross. I'll overcome you, Mr. Devil, through the blood of the Lamb and the word of my testimony! I'll overcome all your attacks!" ∎

CHAPTER EIGHT

Islam In Bible Prophecy

—by Moody Adams

Summary

When Muhammad founded his Islamic faith in the peninsula of Saudi Arabia, there were 360 gods. The most popular god was the "moon god" and we know that because of all the artifacts that have been found. These include a large number of crescent moons, the symbol of the moon god. The name of this moon god was "Allah." This chapter shows how Islam is taking its place in prophecy as a main opponent of Israel and Christianity.

H oward Hill was the greatest archer that ever lived. He never lost a competition. Hill shot charging, wild animals. He killed a shark ten feet under water with his bow and arrow. But in five minutes anyone can learn how to beat this champ shooting the bow. Here is the secret. Blind-fold Howard Hill and turn him around three times. Then it is easy to beat him. Neither Howard Hill, nor any-one else can win unless they can see their target. Outside the arena of archery, it is just as important that a person be focused on the goal if he or she is to be a winner. Jesus said Christians must keep their eyes focused on His return, the consummate goal: *"...look up, and lift up your heads; for your redemption draweth nigh"* (Luke 21:28).

To keep that goal clear and vibrant, we must study Bible prophecies about Christ's return. In Matthew 24, Christ gave us one of the prophecies. The disciples came to him on the Mount of Olives and asked, *"Tell us, when shall these things be? and what shall be the sign of thy coming, and of the end of the world?"* (Matthew 24:3).

Jesus answered, *"...Take heed that no man deceive you.*

"For many shall come in my name, saying, I am Christ; and shall deceive many...

"And many false prophets shall rise, and shall deceive many" (Matthew 24:4 – 5;11).

The first sign Jesus Christ gave and the one He repeated the most often, six times, was "masses being deceived by false teachers." Someone might conclude that this is the pre-eminent sign of the Second Coming of Jesus Christ.

Today, an amazing example of mass religious deception is unfolding. It is being done by the last religion we might ever expect to deceive masses of people—Islam. The religion of Muhammad is the fastest growing in the world. And, for the first time in history, Christianity is no longer the fastest growing religion in America. Islam is.

Islam has succeeded by deception. It is gaining public acceptance despite holding some horrid doctrines:

Islam teaches its followers to kill those who won't accept Islam. It consigns all black-faced men to hell, saying only men with white faces can enter heaven. This religion teaches men to worship "Allah," who can be traced back to the ancient moon god. It orders men to beat their wives. It denounces the deity of Christ, His atonement and His resurrection. Yet, today, a deceived public believes it is one of the greatest world religions, all of which, they wrongly assume, basically teach the same thing!

Islam is growing in America through immigration. A huge number of Muslims are pouring into the United States, legally and illegally, from Canada. It is also growing through reproduction; Muslims are adept at raising large families. They are also opening student worship centers on college campuses to convert young Americans.

Islam is growing by dedicated, aggressive evangelism, especially in the jailhouses of America. Islam is taking the prison system by storm, deceiving masses of prisoners. Muhammad Ali and Mike Tyson are typical examples of thousands of professing Christians who converted to Islam in prisons. In Starke, Florida, two Christian prison chaplains resigned when they were told they would have to stop teaching the Bible and start teaching the Qur'an also.

Islam: Deceiving the Masses About Racism

Most people don't have the faintest idea that Islam is an extremely racist religion. Their successful deception has hidden this fact extremely well. Islam is the only major religion in history that assigns people to heaven or hell on the basis of their skin color.

I went across the ocean and got a computer disk of the two translations of the Qur'an which the Muslims publish.

The Qur'an says in Chapter 3, verses 106,107, that all men with *black* faces will be damned on the day of judgment. Only men with white faces will be saved. Either only white people are going to be accepted by Allah, or black men will have to change their color to white in order to enter heaven.

The Qur'an is the most racist book that has ever been written. Even the KKK has never assigned people to heaven or hell on the basis of skin color like the Qur'an does.

Islam deceives blacks about the fact the founder Muhammad was a racist who actually owned black slaves.

There are two sources of "divine" authority for the Muslims. One is the Qur'an, the other is a set of books called the Hadith. Both are believed to be divinely inspired. Both are believed to be infallible. The Hadith says Muhammad owned black slaves:

> When visiting the home of Muhammad, Umar bin Al-Khattab found that 'a black slave of Allah's apostle was sitting on the first step' (Hadith vol. 6, no. 435).

Other Muslim authorities substantiate that this came after his "divine call." One of Islam's respected scholars wrote:

> Muhammad had many male and female slaves. He used to buy and sell them, but he purchased (more slaves) than he sold, especially after God empowered him by His message ... He (once) sold an black slave for two. His name was Jacob al-Mudbir (Ibn Qayyim al-Jawziyya, Zad al-Ma'ad, Part I, p.160)

Muhammad demeaned blacks as "ugly." He gave Muslims authority to do almost anything they wanted with their female slaves except force them to marry an "ugly" black man:

> But the master doesn't have the right to force the female
> slaves to wed an ugly black slave (Ivn Hazm, Vol. Part 9,
> p.469).

Just try and find a black man holding an office as high as mayor in an Islamic country. You will see how deep Islamic discrimination runs.

In a strange flip-flop, Muslims come over to the United States and declare that Islam is "the religion of blacks," that blacks are superior.

"Nation of Islam" leader Louis Farrakhan says Christianity is the white man's religion; Islam is the black man's religion.

He declares the black man was brought to America and sold into slavery by Jews, by white men. The facts contradict this. African historian J.E. Inikori says it was actually *Arab Muslims* who dominated the slave trade:

> Between the year 650 and 1900, Arab Muslim slave traders
> drained black Africa of 14.4 million black slaves.

In addition to the racism of the Qur'an and the Hadith, "Black Muslim" Louis Farrakhan has added his own racist revelations. He declares black men came to Earth on a spaceship. White men were created by a black scientist who made a mistake in his laboratory. Soon, Farrakhan promises, another space ship is coming to destroy all white men and enable blacks to take over the Earth. Farrakhan, who is really into space ships, says there are 1200 spaceships following him around. One wonders how Farrakhan could pass a sanity hearing if he tried to tell that to a panel of psychiatrists.

Farrakhan doesn't allow white people into his Chicago mosque. He tells his followers to "Get rid of your white slave name and get a black name." So what do they do? They change their names from white Christian names to white Arab slave names. Cassius Clay became Muhammad Ali.

Muhammad was a white man. Muslim scriptures say he was "white" in three different places. Black Muslims tell their people to get rid of the white man's clothes and get some black clothes. They trade white Christian clothes for white Arab clothes, thinking they're actually black clothes!

There is only one place on Earth today where they are selling black slaves: in Muslim countries, particularly in the Sudan. After Louis Farrakhan's public relations visit to his Muslim brothers in the Sudan, a reporter asked him,

> Mr. Farrakhan, why have you been to Sudan, to a country that sells black slaves?

Farrakhan blew up, and screamed, "Bring me proof." Well, two *Baltimore Sun* reporters went over, bought a couple of slaves in the Sudan, and brought them back. We haven't heard anything from Mr. Farrakhan on the subject.

Farrakhan has been to Africa looking for a piece of land. He wants the American government to release all the blacks from prison and relocate them in Africa. This is something like George Wallace proposed in his earlier racist days.

How in the world can Muslims take a Qur'an and stand up and say, "This is the Word of God" and convert black people? The answer is one word, "deception," just what Christ told us would be happening in the last days.

Islam: Deceiving Masses About Moon God Worship
Islam practices idolatry, worshipping the ancient pagan moon god. It has deceived the masses into believing they are worshipping the God of Abraham.

Washington's Mayor Marion Barry, speaking at the Farrakhan "Million Man March," said:

The vision of the Million Man March came directly from God. It was God inspired, whether we call God, 'Jesus Christ,' 'Jehovah,' 'Allah' or just 'God.' He's God.

In other words, Mayor Barry declared, Muslims, Jews and Christians use different names but they all refer to the same God. That is the great deception. In a predominantly Muslim country, you could get killed for saying that. But, when they are trying to proselytize blacks in a Christian country, they put on a deceptive face.

When Muhammad founded his Islamic faith in the peninsula of Saudi Arabia, there were 360 gods. The most popular was the moon god and we know that because of all the artifacts that have been found. These include a large number of crescent moons, the symbols of the moon god. The name of this moon god was "Allah."

Just look on the top of the Muslim mosques and towers. There you will see the crescent moon, the symbol of the moon god. Muslims put the crescent moon on their prayer cloths. You can listen to them chanting "Allah!"

Muslims tell Westerners they are worshipping the same God as Jews and Christians. They are not. They are merely trying to deceive people about their worship of the pagan moon god. They say, "We worship the God of Abraham." Look at how successful their deception has been. Catholics have re-written their doctrine to say that Muslims will go to heaven because they are worshipping the God of Abraham. The deceptive forces of Islam sold them on it!

Islam tells people their Scriptures are the inspired word of Allah. But there are many things they don't obey and certainly don't talk about.

Islam Says Kill Dogs and Drink Camel Urine

For instance, their Scriptures command followers to "Kill all dogs" (Hadith, vol. 4, no. 539, 540). Muhammad didn't like dogs nipping at his heels. He conveniently got a revelation from his god ordering all dogs killed. Muslims hide this command from their "holy scripture."

Then, when followers get sick, Allah orders them to drink milk and camel urine (Hadith, volume 1, #234). Muslims hide this, also. I often ask Muslims, when they confront me, if they really believe the Qur'an and the Hadith. When they say, "yes," I challenge them to prove it by killing all the town's dogs and drinking some camel urine!

Islam Says That Jesus Was a Lying Blasphemer

In 1996, I went in to speak at a church in Okeechobe, Florida, and discovered the first two rows were filled with Muslims in full Islamic dress. They behaved while I gave my sermon, but at the end, they stood up and strongly challenged me. For two-and-a-half hours, we debated. These included doctors and prominent people. The Okeechobe Christians were startled. They had no idea Islam was so strong in their remote community. They were even more startled that these people would blatantly come in and attack the deity of Jesus Christ.

Islam says it is idolatry to worship Jesus. They teach it is blasphemy to say He was God in a human body. They declare Christ didn't die on the cross and that He wasn't raised for our justification.

They try to deceive uninformed Christians by saying, "We believe in Jesus Christ." And they do. But they believe that He was just another prophet.

A Muslim imam [a preacher of the Islamic faith] told me, "Moses was a prophet. Abraham was a prophet. Jesus was a prophet. But Muhammad was the last prophet. To be saved, you must renounce Jesus Christ, all other prophets and embrace Muhammad, the final prophet."

Islam: Deceiving the Masses About Abuse of Women
Islamic deception has reached all the way to the White House in Washington, D.C. I really felt sorry for our President's wife, Mrs. Hillary Clinton. She is a very educated woman, but of course, she couldn't be expected to know much about Islam.

Mrs. Clinton had the first Islamic meeting ever held in the White House on February 20th, 1996. This coincided with the end of Ramadan, the Muslim "high holy day."

She invited 150 Muslims, including Chaplain Muhammad, the first Muslim cleric to be put on the payroll of the U.S. Government. They presented Mrs. Clinton with a copy of the Qur'an. Mrs. Clinton responded by praising Islam's contribution to the family, saying,

> The values of life, the heart of Islam, faith, family, community, and responsibility to the less fortunate, resonates with all the people of the Earth.

If Mrs. Clinton ever gets around to reading the Qur'an Chaplain Muhammad gave her, she could be a very embarrassed First Lady. It says a man is to beat his wife:

> As for those women, on whose part she feels disloyalty, and ill conduct, admonish them, refuse to share their beds and beat them, banish them to beds apart and scourge them (Qur'an 4:34).

This requires more than just an ordinary beating—the Arabic implies that it means "a scourging." A scourge is a whip with several strips of leather; often a little metal and bone is added to the throngs. If you have wondered how the Muslim men can handle four wives, the scourge is the key.

Islam tries to explain this by putting out a special doctored English edition that says, "beat them lightly." But the Arabic word in the Qur'an for scourging wives is the same word used for scourging criminals.

Islam allows a woman only half the vote of the man on a jury. A woman only gets half of the inheritance of a man. A woman has to walk 10 feet behind the man. Paul Harvey reported they've changed that in Kuwait. Now the women are walking 10 feet *in front* of the man because of the land mines left by the Iraqis.

Islam gives women no security in their marriages. In chapter 2, verse 36 of the Qur'an, it says, "It is no sin for you to divorce women."

The 2nd chapter, verses 229–230, say that to get a permanent divorce, all you have to do is say,

I divorce you, I divorce you, I divorce you.

This three word phrase, repeated three times, finishes the marriage forever.

Islam is vehemently against sex outside of marriage. But, Muslim men can go into a house of prostitution, marry a girl and then say "I divorce you" three times as they leave. This is Islamic morality.

I went into the largest mosque in America, the one in New York City. I had a video camera with me and interviewed the top imam in America, who had come here from the world's largest university in Cairo, Egypt.

I said, "You practice having multiple wives."

"Yes," he replied. "But what you must understand—

Muslims are very, very moral people. Here in America, if a Christian marries a woman, he lives with her for a few months and then he sees another woman and he would like to have her. What does the Christian do? He sneaks around and has an affair with her. Not Muslims.

"What the Muslim does when he sees another woman he likes, he marries her.

"But Muslims are very moral, very fair. If you give a gift to one wife, you have to give one to all your wives. If you sleep with one wife, you have to sleep with all the other wives also. We are very, very moral."

The Islamic treatment of women is accurately and vividly displayed in the movie, "Not Without My Daughter" starring Sally Field. This is a true story of a woman who is now lecturing all across the United States of America. She married an Islamic doctor she met in college. He tricked her into taking a vacation to his home and wouldn't let her leave.

In a devout Muslim society, a woman cannot take a bus, train, or plane without her husband's permission. It was through miraculous help that this woman managed to escape.

Every parent and grandparent should have a burning commitment to get the truth about Islam to their daughters and granddaughters. This is particularly true if the young girls are going off to college, where they might meet a charming young Muslim man with a lot of money.

Islam: Deceiving the Masses About Murder

When a Christian murders, he is refusing to follow Jesus Christ and is disobeying the Bible. When a Muslim kills, he is following Muhammad's example and obeying the Qur'an. The religion of Islam was fathered by a murderer, born in a sea of innocent blood, and spread by an army of vicious and merciless killers. Today, Islamic Scriptures give repeated reasons why every Muslim should be a murderer.

Muhammad raised up an army which soaked the Arabian peninsula in blood. He overthrew the government. That pattern continues in Iran, Egypt, the Sudan, Pakistan and Turkey, where Muslims are killing to overthrow their governments and establish an Islamic fundamentalist state.

Muhammad himself killed without hesitation:

> When Muhammad was told that Ibn Khatal was taking
> refuge in the Kabah, he ordered, 'Kill him.' He was
> butchered. (Hadith, vol. 3, no. 72).

Muhammad gave the world the Qur'an which commands Muslims to kill all those who refuse to accept Islam:

> But when the forbidden months are past, they fight and slay
> the Pagans wherever ye find them, and seize them, beleaguer
> them, and lie in wait for them in every stratagem (of war),
> but if they repent, and establish regular prayers and practice
> regular charity, then open way for them: for God is oft-for-
> giving, Most merciful (Qur'an 9:5).

The Qur'an commands Muslims to kill anyone who tries to leave the religion of Islam:

> If they turn back (to enmity) then take them and kill them
> wherever ye find them (Qur'an 4:89). On August 6, 1977,
> the Egyptian newspaper al-Ahram reported the government
> had voted the death penalty for apostasy—leaving the
> Islamic religion.

The only way a Muslim can have assurance of heaven is to die killing people for Allah. Even Muhammad said he didn't know whether he would go to heaven when he died. He said it all depended on what mood Allah was in that day. But, if you die killing people for Allah you are *assured* of heaven:

> Think not of those who were slain in the way of God as
> dead. Nay, they are alive, finding their sustenance with their
> Lord (Qur'an 3:169).

Plus, they are promised couches of silk brocade, surrounded by all manner of fruit and virgin girls. The nude virgin girls are conveniently chained, unable to resist any advance. This is what motivates the young Muslim terrorists who hope to land on a couch of pleasure with a virgin by blowing up Jewish women and children in Jerusalem. This was the motivation of the Muslim terrorists who bombed the New York World Trade Center.

We can expect more terrorism by Muslims in America. Libyan dictator Muamar Gadhafi, who has given Louis Farrakhan millions of dollars to fund the Black Muslim cause in America, said:

> Our confrontation with America was like a fight against a
> fortress from outside, and today we found a breach to enter
> into the fortress and confront it.

According to an FBI agent, the two most radical, destructive terrorist groups in the Muslim world are working actively in the United States. They are raising money and training killers in the land that affords them more freedom than any other.

Every mosque in the world teaches the Qur'an and every Qur'an commands Muslims to fight those who don't believe in Allah and kill them when they can.

A lot of Muslims are good citizens who have been deceived by a murderous religion. The problem lies in the demonic doctrines of the religion. One of Farrakhan's aides, his militia commander, said in Atlanta,

> I don't ask if you are willing to die for Allah, I want to know
> if you are willing to kill for Allah?

This is the problem with Muslim teaching in America.

What We Must Do
The Bible told us false prophets would come, deceiving many. We need to be aware of what our enemy is doing. We must not be ignorant of the Devil's devices.

We need to work to protect our children and grandchildren from this deceptive religion. We need to get out and work harder to win people to the truth.

We need to make a deeper commitment. It breaks my heart when I look outside the factories and plants and see Muslims in their suits and ties giving out their literature, working, smiling.

I don't see any Christians outside those factories and plants. It is time we wake up and get this message out before it is too late.

Above all else, the rise of Islam means prophecy is being fulfilled. God is on the throne, Jesus is coming and we should be rejoicing!

God is able to give victory in the midst of all our troubles. Christ said, *"And when these things begin to come to pass, then look up, and lift up your heads; for your redemption draweth nigh"* (Luke 21:28).

The favorite song of the prisoners on death row in the Philippines is, "Soon and very soon, we are going to see the King!" Christ can put a joyful expectation in the heart of a man awaiting execution. So, certainly, He can fill us with His joy in the midst of the problems we are facing.

This is a blessed, joyful, hope. Look up. Stay focused on the goal. Christ is coming! ∎

CHAPTER NINE

How To Be A Winner In the Last Days

—by Moody Adams

Summary

Its not too late to win. Stand up to your enemy and all of his hissing, laughing, mocking, and all the reasons you've got to fail. Believe God like Samson did: bring down the enemy's stronghold! Go out a winner!

This chapter will give you a vigorous inspiration to face the challenges ahead. God is on your side as you draw near to Him!

Any Christian can be a winner, even in the midst of all the evils of the last days. The Bible shows exactly how to be a victorious, triumphant Christian even when facing all of hell's furies.

While it is possible to win, it isn't easy. Scripture says the last days will be marked by "perilous times" (2nd Timothy 3:1–5). The human race will advance in terms of knowledge, but morally, *"...evil men and seducers shall wax worse and worse, deceiving, and being deceived"* (2nd Timothy 3:13).

Jesus foretold that Christians would be despised and persecuted, *"Then shall they deliver you up to be afflicted, and shall kill you: and ye shall be hated of all nations for my name's sake"* (Matthew 24:9).

But God has given us a pattern of victory, a man we can follow to be winners. His name is Samson. He lived in perilous, evil times. The godless Philistines were set upon destroying him and his people. Samson's life was in daily peril, yet, he was strong.

Samson had been called by God before his birth to be the leader of the Jewish people. He was ordained to lead his nation to victory over the enemy—the Philistines. Samson seemed to have the great physical strength for his task. In fact, once he killed a lion with his bare hands.

When his enemies thought they had him trapped, he jumped up and carried off the city gates. When an army surrounded him, Samson took the jawbone of a donkey and slew them.

For years after his death, poets wrote of him and singers sang about the mighty Samson. Though thousands of years have passed, when the Madison Avenue marketing experts today want to convey strength for a product, they use the name of Samson: Samsonite luggage, Samsun locks. The name still resonates strength.

Picture Samson standing on the pedestal of greatness. See his mighty muscles. Hear the cheers that rise from his people. Feel the admiration, respect and praise that filled his life. Sense the destiny of a divine call to liberate your nation. Just look at him, the strongest man who had ever lived.

Now call upon your imagination and take a trip with me. Place yourself in the ancient land of Gaza. This is the slave capital of the world. Walk down the streets of this depraved city and look at men herded and sold like cattle.

Come with me to the most horrible place in this horrid land, the prison house. You can smell it before you see it because the bodies of the dead lay mingled with the living. Hold your breath and step into this dungeon of despair. Hear the sullen moans and hollowed groans of a thousand tortured ghosts.

Feel the hopelessness in this sea of ruined lives. Look down at the gaunt form of what had once been a man. Now, there is only a skeleton with skin stretched over it. See the back scarred from the bitter cuts of the jailer's whip. Look on the repulsive sores which mark the spots where they prodded him with sharp sticks. Grotesque rings of ulcers mark the places the brass cuffs circled his arms. This tortured ghost felt all the pain of his tormentors, but he didn't see them.

The Philistines guaranteed their prisoners wouldn't give them trouble by running a sharp dagger beside the nose and flipping the eyeballs out with one quick twist of the blade. It is hard for you to even look at the hollow holes where the keen eyes used to be. But force yourself to look and face the stark reality that this is the wretched form of Samson. In all the history of the world, no man ever fell from such great heights of victory to such despicable depths of defeat.

The Bible records this wasn't the end of his suffering, *"Then the lords of the Philistines gathered them together for*

*to offer a great sacrifice unto Dagon their god, and to
rejoice: for they said, Our god hath delivered Samson our
enemy into our hand.*

*"And when the people saw him, they praised their god:
for they said, Our god hath delivered into our hands our
enemy, and the destroyer of our country, which slew many
of us.*

*"And it came to pass, when their hearts were merry, that
they said, Call for Samson, that he may make us sport. And
they called for Samson out of the prison house; and he made
them sport: and they set him between the pillars"* (Judges
16:23–25).

To all Samson's physical torture, they added the pain of
shame, ridicule and mockery. They boasted of how superior
their god, "Dagon," was. The disgrace was more torturous
than their beatings. Samson suffered the shame of his folly
and fall.

But wait. There is a startling end to the story:

*"And Samson said unto the lad that held him by the hand,
Suffer me that I may feel the pillars whereupon the house
standeth, that I may lean upon them.*

*"Now the house was full of men and women; and all the
lords of the Philistines were there; and there were upon the
roof about three thousand men and women, that beheld
while Samson made sport.*

*"And Samson called unto the LORD, and said, O Lord
GOD, remember me, I pray thee, and strengthen me, I pray
thee, only this once, O God, that I may be at once avenged
of the Philistines for my two eyes.*

*"And Samson took hold of the two middle pillars upon
which the house stood, and on which it was borne up, of the
one with his right hand, and of the other with his left."*

Can you see him now, leaning up against the pillars,
where he starts praying? And can you can imagine the roar

as they screamed in ridicule, "Look! Samson is going to push the pillars down!"

But now, listen. Samson continues his prayer:

"Let me die with the Philistines. And he bowed himself with all his might; and the house fell upon the lords, and upon all the people that were therein. So the dead which he slew at his death were more than they which he slew in his life" (Judges 16:26–30).

That day, Samson dealt a death blow to the Philistines. Their leadership was destroyed; their nation didn't recover. The Jews were freed from their oppressors as Samson fulfilled the task Almighty God ordained him for. In his weakness, Samson became stronger than he had ever been before, and in his death, Samson became a greater victor than he had been in all his years of strength.

Through 3,000 years of history, Samson is screaming at us, "It isn't too late to be a winner!" I don't care how low you have sunk, how weak you have become, how hopeless the battle looks, it isn't to late to win!

Here are Samson's two keys to winning:

First, you must pray to God for power. *Second,* you must demonstrate your faith.

Samson prayed and took hold of the pillars. He demonstrated his faith that God was going to answer his prayer.

You Can Win Over the People Who Oppose You

Perhaps you have been beaten down by cruel people. The Bible says in the last days, the love of many is going to wax cold. You may have already experienced this. People may have torn your heart out. Those you work for may have shown little appreciation. The children you raised may have neglected you. The mate you gave your life to may have grown indifferent. You can imagine how Samson felt. Every time he gave his love to others, they ended up breaking his heart. The woman he was engaged to sold him out in sport. Then, there was Delilah whom he loved. She betrayed him, sold him out to the Philistines, and was responsible for his capture and the gouging of his eyes. He was a complete failure, it seemed.

Remember Samson. Even if people have turned against you and broken your heart, you can be a winner.

My greatest human hero, next to the Apostle Paul, is John Wesley. He was a tremendous man of God, whom secular historians say saved England from the fate of France [the humanistic and murderous French Revolution] and impacted two continents for Christ.

I love to go to his church and study John Wesley. A very disciplined man, he kept a journal and wouldn't go to sleep at night until he brought it up to date. Wesley would write how much time he had spent in prayer, how many sermons he had preached. He usually preached seven a day, but cut back to two a day when he was on vacation.

He would write down the sins he had committed that day and confess them. Wesley said when he closed his journal at night, he did so as if the next time his record was opened it would be at the judgment seat of Christ.

Though he wrote about his life in great detail, he never mentioned one thing: his troubles with his wife.

Sam Jones, a great old war horse evangelist, was preaching a crusade once and a man came up to him and said, "John, people here don't like your preaching. You've upset everybody in town. The people are really criticizing you."

Sam raised his hands up to heaven and said "Praise God, I don't mind being swallowed by a whale, but I hate to be nibbled to death by these minnows."

Put your enemies in perspective. They can nibble on you and irritate you, but they cannot defeat you. They are not nearly as big as your Lord. You are on a mission from

Almighty God. God put you here for these times. He placed you here to be a winner. If people support you, fine. If they turn against you, keep going and believe God can make you a winner.

John Wesley married late in life. Things didn't go well in the marriage. Wesley may not have been the best husband in the world, but his wife had some serious problems.

One time, Wesley was standing up preaching to thousands in a town square in London on the subject of liquor. Wesley's wife cried out from the middle of the audience, "Ain't he a fine one and at daybreak he was too drunk to turn over in bed."

A critic of John Wesley, who would never have told anything in his favor, said he once went to the house to see Wesley and found the large Mrs. Wesley dragging her husband by the hair across the floor. Yet in all of his writings, Wesley never mentioned any of this.

Every time I hear a preacher say, "I think I am going to have to get out of the ministry because my wife isn't supportive," I think up in heaven John Wesley must say, "Give me a microscope and let me look at this little creature down there who calls himself a preacher."

God used Wesley to change his world and He carried him through the great rejection by his wife.

You have to stand, by faith, like Samson. Believe you can win even if people have turned against you. If you have friends and a supportive family, thank God. But if everyone turns against you, you can still be a winner, even in these loveless, last days.

The Bible says, *"What shall we then say to these things? If God be for us, who can be against us?"* (Romans 8:31). Repeat this every day, *"If God be for us, who can be against us?"* Shout it out to the Devil, *"If God be for us, who can be against us?"*

You Can Win Despite Your Handicaps

It is tempting for some to say, "I cannot win because of my handicap." But I have some handicaps. Don't we all? Everyone's circumstances have some disadvantages, but everyone also has some gifts, some talent and some potential. Samson was blind when he performed his mightiest act!

Two men got polio. One of them sat on a street corner in New York and begged for money. The other became President of the United States—Franklin Delano Roosevelt.

You Can Win Without Ability

Some easily exclude themselves from the winner's circle by saying, "I am just not qualified to do anything very important." This is why it can be real fun being on the committee that picks a church's Sunday School teachers.

People will say, "Oh, I would love to take that job, but I am just not qualified. You'll have to find somebody else." That's when the fun begins.

You reply, "Well, let's see how qualified you are. God has an aptitude test right here which says:

"For ye see your calling, brethren, how that not many wise men after the flesh, not many mighty, not many noble, are called:

"But God hath chosen the foolish things of the world to confound the wise; and God hath chosen the weak things of the world to confound the things which are mighty;

"And base things of the world, and things which are despised, hath God chosen, yea, and things which are not, to bring to nought things that are:

"That no flesh should glory in his presence" (1st Corinthians 1:26–29).

Here are the five questions on God's aptitude test:

1—Are you foolish?

2—Are you weak?

3—Are you a base, low-down person?
4—Are you despised?
5—Are you an absolute nothing?

If you can answer "Yes" to these things, you are exactly who God is looking for. Why? So that *"no flesh should glory in His presence!"*

If you are a great orator, a great writer, a great personality, or a great talent, people will say, "Isn't he wonderful!"

But when somebody who doesn't have all this ability, somebody handicapped by lack of talent, someone who is weak, foolish, and despised does it, people will say, "I don't understand it. He isn't anything. God must be in it."

You think you're limited by a lack of ability? Look at poor Samson laying there in the prison. He was beat to a pulp, starved nearly to death and blind. What could he possibly do for Almighty God? He could save a nation and immortalize his name, that's what he could do!

You Can Win In Spite of Handicaps, Despite Weakness
Perhaps you feel too weak to win against all the discouragements, temptations and trials facing you. Remember, Samson couldn't really trust God until all his strength was gone.

The Bible says in Hebrews 11:34, "Out of weakness" the champions "were made strong." When I was preaching on this in North Carolina, I asked the folks in the congregation to name their biggest problems. One lady got up and really nailed me. She said, "How do you deal with sickness?"

I didn't like that question. You see, I don't handle sickness very well. When I get sick, I want to lay down and whine. I want my wife to come "mama" me, to say, "Poor baby, you're feeling so bad." I just eat that up. I love it. But this characteristic I have is really disappointing, because

I've always aspired to be like Paul. He said, *"...of myself I will not glory, but in mine infirmities.*

"For though I would desire to glory, I shall not be a fool; for I will say the truth: but now I forbear, lest any man should think of me above that which he seeth me to be, or that he heareth of me.

"And lest I should be exalted above measure through the abundance of the revelations, there was given to me a thorn in the flesh, the messenger of Satan to buffet me, lest I should be exalted above measure.

"For this thing I besought the Lord thrice, that it might depart from me.

"And he said unto me, My grace is sufficient for thee: for my strength is made perfect in weakness. Most gladly therefore will I rather glory in my infirmities, that the power of Christ may rest upon me.

"Therefore I take pleasure in infirmities, in reproaches, in necessities, in persecutions, in distresses for Christ's sake: for when I am weak, then am I strong" (2nd Corinthians 12:5–10).

Paul took pleasure in being sick.

He said, in effect, "I love to be sick. I glory in it. When I get sick, it is so exciting, you know, I just glory in it when my body is aching and I don't feel good. I glory in it."

Why? Well, Paul said in effect, "When I am weak, that's when God is strongest in me."

We human beings normally won't put our faith in God until there isn't anything else left to trust in. We have got to come to the end of ourselves before we can come to the beginning of God. We have to reach the absolute end of our strength before we get to the beginning of God's strength.

God couldn't use Samson until all of his strength was gone. Only then in his frailty did he put all his trust in the Lord's power.

Look up today and say, "God, I am weak, but you are strong. God, renew my strength just this one time." In your weakness you will experience the power of God's Holy Spirit. It isn't too late for you to be a winner, no matter how weak you may be.

You Can Win Despite Past Failures

You may say, "But I've tried. You don't know how many times I've tried. I've tried and I've failed." Well, Samson tried and tried and became an absolute failure. But finally, in the power of God, he won.

We can learn some important lessons from sports. That's why God used sports analogies in the Bible. Paul buffeting and boxing his body, the writer of Hebrews talking about running the race.

I heard a man tell about his aspiration to be a runner. As a lad, he trained hard and perspired and worked and put in all the hours necessary to good training.

When his first race came, he lost. He went back and worked harder. Then he ran again and lost. Afterward, he lost and lost and lost.

You know, at some point and time you have got to face reality and give up, right?

Well, didn't. He kept going even after he had lost 45 straight races. The man's name is Carl Lewis. He will, no doubt, go down as the greatest track athlete of our times!

I love to watch basketball player Michael Jordan because every time I see him, I think of that day when he stood there with great hopes as his coach wrote the names of the boys in his school that had made the basketball team.

Michael's name wasn't on it! He went home and laid across the bed and cried.

But he didn't quit. He got up and became the greatest basketball player in history!

Boxer Muhammad Ali said the secret of winning is just to get up one time more than you get knocked down. That is what athletes can teach Christians.

I am wounded, Sir Galahad said, I am wounded, but I am not slain, I will lay me down and bleed a while, then I will fight again.

That is it. You must realize that failure isn't final. There is still time to win.

Colonel Sanders was 65 years old, retired, and living on a small pension. Then, he started Kentucky Fried Chicken. I wish we could start missions as fast as they are opening Kentucky Fried Chicken outlets. The restaurants are in practically every country all over the world. Sanders didn't even start the business until he was 65. When he was in his 70's, he got saved. In his 80's, if you would let him get up and give his testimony, you would have to physically pull him off the platform. He would never quit.

Abraham never amounted to anything until that day, when he was 100 years old, he came limping out of the house crying, "Its a boy! Sarah had a boy!" From that moment on, he was off and running. If you are under 100, it is certainly not too late to be a winner!

I beg of you to do one thing: Put your hands upon the pillars of your enemies, those things that have come against you. Put your hands on the pillars of your opposition. Pray, "God strengthen me." Go out and be a winner!

Martin Luther, the great reformer, stood against the tides of public opinion. He stood against the mighty Roman Catholic Church because it was charging people money in order to get to heaven.

Martin Luther had a personal weakness. He was afflicted by depression. When he got discouraged, he would go in his room and shut himself up. Sometimes, he wouldn't come out. He wouldn't talk to people and he wouldn't eat. Luther had good reason to be discouraged. The Catholics were hunting him to kill him.

One day, when it looked like everything in his Protestant effort was lost and the Catholics were going to destroy him and his cause of telling men salvation was a free gift, Luther got so depressed that he went in the room and wouldn't come out. Nobody could cheer him up. He felt it was all hopeless. He gave up and laid there on the floor for about a week.

Then he heard the door to the room open and he looked up. There was a woman dressed in black: black hat, black veil, black dress, black gloves; the dress of mourning for the dead. It was his wife. Forgetting his own sorrows for a moment, he said, "Someone's dead?"

"Yes, Luther," his wife replied.

"Who is dead?"

His wife answered, "God is dead."

Luther angrily shouted, "Woman, shut up! Don't you know it's blasphemy to talk like that?"

His wife replied, "Martin Luther, if it's blasphemy for me to talk like God's dead, then it's blasphemy for you live like God's dead."

Martin Luther got up off that floor and went out and tore down the pillars of his enemy. The Protestant Reformation won. The world would hear that salvation was a free gift. Luther went out a victor.

Its not too late to win. Stand up to your enemy and all of his hissing and laughing and mocking, and all the reasons you've got to fail. Believe God like Samson did: bring down the enemy's stronghold. Go out a winner! ∎

CHAPTER TEN

The Beast From the Abyss

—by Dr. David Webber

Summary

"The beast that thou sawest was, and is not; and shall ascend out of the bottom-less pit, and go into perdition: and they that dwell on the earth shall wonder, whose names were not written in the book of life from the foundation of the world, when they behold the beast that was, and is not, and yet is."

The Beast is the final world ruler, the Antichrist who deceives all nations into believing he is the Christ, the savior of the world. The Devil lied in the Garden of Eden when he said that Adam and Eve could become like God.

My text is Revelation 17:8, *"The beast that thou sawest was, and is not; and shall ascend out of the bottomless pit, and go into perdition: and they that dwell on the earth shall wonder, whose names were not written in the book of life from the foundation of the world, when they behold the beast that was, and is not, and yet is."*

I believe this verse indicates that the Beast will be a walking "dead man," someone who has come back from the realm of the dead in a corruptible body.

As part of the "mystery of iniquity," there are other Scriptures that could indicate this.

In contra-distinction to Christ, who arose from the dead in a glorified body after three days and three nights in the grave, the Scriptures declare that death has no more dominion over Him.

"But now is Christ risen from the dead, and become the firstfruits of them that slept.

"For since by man came death, by man came also the resurrection of the dead.

"For as in Adam all die, even so in Christ shall all be made alive" (1st Corinthians 15:20–22).

"Forasmuch then as the children are partakers of flesh and blood, he also himself likewise took part of the same; that through death he might destroy him that had the power of death, that is, the devil;

"And deliver them who through fear of death were all their lifetime subject to bondage" (Hebrews 2:14,15).

Because "the wages of sin is death," why couldn't the Devil call forth a selected person to come back from the

silent halls of death as his appointed ruler for the last days—
the Antichrist?

In one of the earliest books of the Old Testament, the
Book of Job, there are passages that certainly point to such
a conclusion:

*"Terrors shall make him afraid on every side, and shall
drive him to his feet.*

*"His strength shall be hungerbitten, and destruction shall
be ready at his side.*

*"It shall devour the strength of his skin: even the firstborn
of death shall devour his strength.*

*"His confidence shall be rooted out of his tabernacle, and
it shall bring him to the king of terrors.*

*"It shall dwell in his tabernacle, because it is none of his:
brimstone shall be scattered upon his habitation.*

*"His roots shall be dried up beneath, and above shall his
branch be cut off.*

*"His remembrance shall perish from the earth, and he
shall have no name in the street.*

*"He shall be driven from light into darkness, and chased
out of the world.*

*"He shall neither have son nor nephew among his peo-
ple, nor any remaining in his dwellings.*

*"They that come after him shall be astonied at his day, as
they that went before were affrighted.*

*"Surely such are the dwellings of the wicked, and this is
the place of him that knoweth not God"* (Job 18:11–21).

This is possibly a prophecy for the Antichrist: a walking
dead man who will return to the place of the dead!

*"In the fulness of his sufficiency he shall be in straits:
every hand of the wicked shall come upon him.*

*"When he is about to fill his belly, God shall cast the fury
of his wrath upon him, and shall rain it upon him while he
is eating.*

"He shall flee from the iron weapon, and the bow of steel shall strike him through.

"It is drawn, and cometh out of the body; yea, the glittering sword cometh out of his gall: terrors are upon him.

"All darkness shall be hid in his secret places: a fire not blown shall consume him; it shall go ill with him that is left in his tabernacle.

"The heaven shall reveal his iniquity; and the earth shall rise up against him.

"The increase of his house shall depart, and his goods shall flow away in the day of his wrath.

"This is the portion of a wicked man from God, and the heritage appointed unto him by God" (Job 20:22–29).

This could indicate an assassination attempt will come upon Antichrist at a banquet. But the whole world will be astonished! You can't kill a dead man. He's already dead!

Zechariah 11:17 gives us some insight that the deadly attack will fall upon his right eye and his arm.

"Woe to the idol shepherd that leaveth the flock! the sword shall be upon his arm, and upon his right eye: his arm shall be clean dried up, and his right eye shall be utterly darkened" (Zechariah 11:17).

Regarding the Antichrist, how will his short-lived empire operate?

Revelation 13:15–17 indicates that it will be a system of marks and numbers, basically a cashless society of credit cards, debit cards, and sophisticated computer operation.

Is such a system feasible today? Yes! We will provide you an example from *U.S.A. Today*, September 18, 1995. A cover story titled, "First Data deal may bring us closer to a cashless society," reported:

> When you use a credit card or debit card, check your credit
> card balance or get a credit card bill, chances are your

transaction was touched by First Data. The same goes if you call collect on MCI, phone Dreyfus or another mutual fund company about your account, pay a utility bill at a convenience store, send a money order or wire money to a relative.

First Data's Omaha operations are the heart and soul of a $736–billion-a-year world-wide market for payment-card processing. What happens here and in other First Data buildings in 131 cities in the USA, the United Kingdom, Australia and Mexico is becoming increasingly vital to the lives of millions of consumers everywhere.

I wouldn't say the world would end if First Data went out of business tomorrow, but consumers would sure as heck notice, says William Rabin of J.P. Morgan. We'd all have to start writing checks and using cash again.

Ten miles from First Data's Omaha card-service center is the war room, a command center that easily could be mistaken for an air traffic control center. Behind walls designed to withstand tornadoes and even Earthquakes—which rarely occur here—is the computer data center that provides around-the-clock technical advice and service to banks that issue credit cards and to merchants who accept the cards. Workers staff rows of computer terminals. On the walls before them, huge screens monitor credit-card activity of banks and merchants.

First Data handles just about everything needed to make, book and process financial transactions electronically. It reviews credit applications, checks credit references, records credit-card purchases at the point of sale, speeds a record of sales to banks, keeps track of a customer's payment record and prints and mails credit-card bills.

In the center, each laser printer spits out credit-card statements—on 1,800 different forms with different mailing logos—at a rate of 244 pages a minute, seven days a week, 24 hours a day. The printers consume 55 million linear feet of paper a month, up from 30 million five years ago. Statements pass through 17 checkpoints before they get to machines that sort them by zip code and prepare them to be delivered by the U.S. Postal Service. First Data accounts for one in every 4.5 letters mailed in Omaha.

The computer center is bigger than a football field. Most of it is filled with data storage silos that contain more than 200,000 computer tapes. The silos contain information on 92 million credit cards processed last year—up from 44 million in 1989. You can walk blocks before bumping into a human being.

Across town, in the plastics process center, there are plenty of people. And they treat the plastic cards as if they were gold. Here are row after row and box after box of 24,000 types of cards, representing thousands of issuers. Among them: some of the nation's largest banks, oil companies and retailers.

But First Data won't disclose names because some contracts won't allow it. One bank may have as many as 3,000 versions of a card, naming the cities in which it operates.

Because First Data knows that even an honest person might be tempted to pocket a few cards, every card in the building is counted once a month. Employees work in pairs. They track the movement of cards by computer and sign in and out whenever they move a card from the vault to a machine that prints account numbers and customer names. Precision is essential.

Random quality inspections are made to ensure cards are 3.3 inches long by 2.1 inches wide. Tolerances are measured in thousandths of an inch.

Brinks security trucks pick up blank cards from suppliers and deliver them to this factory. The building is so secret and the operations so sensitive that *U.S.A. TODAY* wasn't allowed to take photographs inside.

Until recently, the services provided by Fist Data and other credit card processing companies were virtually ignored—except by merchants, banks and financial services companies. And that's the way First Data wants it.

If we do our job right, consumers won't even know we exist, says John Elliott, First Data's strategic adviser.

But by year's end, First Data probably will be too big for consumers to ignore. By then, it expects to have completed its acquisition of rival First Financial Management.

The $6.6 billion deal, announced in June 1995, will combine the nation's two largest financial payment processors. Together, they'll have annual revenue of $4 billion, net income of more than $400 million.

First Data will be even more involved—and know even more about—the way consumers spend money and pay with plastic.

The size, scope and power of the new First Data is stunning to Wall Street. And in one business—wiring money around the world for consumers—First Data would simply be too big and too powerful, federal regulators decided. At the insistence of the Federal Trade Commission, First Data agreed to spin off the sales and marketing operations of First Financial's Western Union unit which controls 90% of the money-wiring market-or First Data's Money Gram unit, which controls the rest of the market. The spin-off is expected to resolve any antitrust problems.

The deal means that the much-hyped cashless society— when electronic financial transactions virtually replace the use of cash and checks—that's been talked about for decades, may be closer. Our combined resources should help make reality many of the things people have only dreamed of for years, says First Data's Elliott.

A cashless society still seems a long way off. In 1996, U.S. consumers wrote 58 billion checks, and electronic

payments accounted for just 16% of the $5.2 trillion payment
market—a market expected to grow to $8.5 trillion by 2000.

But increasingly, consumers are proving their penchant
for doing business electronically. Most spend more time at
automated teller machines than in bank branches. A decade
ago, less than 5% of U.S. consumers had paychecks directly
deposited into bank accounts. Now, 40% use direct deposit.

But can First Data make the cashless society happen?
Industry experts say they have the tools. In this business, the
one with the lowest cost per transaction and the most efficient operation wins, says Rabin, who ran J.P. Morgan's
computer systems before becoming an analyst. I was flabber-
gasted with how efficient First Data's technology and operations in Omaha are.

A new check-cashing machine has recently been installed in
Oklahoma City that demonstrates how this electronic technology is speeding at incredible rates down the super information highway.

An article in *Dave Webber Reports*, December 1997, enti-
tled "The ATM Path to the Mark of the Beast," states:

> Automation is making life easier; now you don't have to go
> to the bank to cash a check. I'm quoting *The Daily
> Oklahoman*, September 26, 1997. The story was titled,
> Store's Machine Can Cash Checks.
>
>   Oklahoma City has the state's first automated check-cash-
> ing machine, the latest development in self-serve, banking
> gadgetry. Fort Worth, Texas-based Mr. Payroll Corp.,
> through local franchisee Hawk Enterprises, recently installed
> the machine at the 7–Eleven store at SE 44th and Shields.
>
>   The machine looks like an ATM; can accommodate
> English-or Spanish-speaking users and cashes most kinds of
> checks for fees ranging from 1% to 3% of the face amounts.

The Oklahoma City machine is one of only seven. Most are in the Dallas-Fort Worth area.

'We do plan to deploy others there in the future, Mr. Payroll President Michael Stinson said.

Demand for the machines should grow, he said, especially at banks looking for ways to cut costs by reducing the number of transactions that require live tellers.

Patrons operate the machine by touching commands on the screen and entering their Social Security numbers. A camera inside the machine takes their photographs.

First-time patrons are directed to an attached telephone receiver to verify their identities with a Fort Worth operator by answering personal questions that each Social Security number holder should know.

During subsequent visits, the machine can verify identities without the operator by comparing the image of the person at the machine with an image stowed away electronically.

The machine spits out the checks of those whose identities don't match, but the check casher can actually keep a check that's a potential forgery.

Mr. Payroll's Oklahoma City machine already has helped nab one forger, said Stephen Lerdall, a Hawk Enterprises representative.

Lerdall said he's also seen the machine reject several others who didn't match the identities of the check recipients.

The machine subtracts a 1% fee for cashing payroll and government checks, 2% for tax and insurance checks, and 3% for personal and two-party checks.

Although its too early to project revenue, Stinson said the machines already cash as many as 120 checks on busy days.

Mr. Payroll has operated manned check-cashing kiosks inside stores for seven years. However, the machines eventually could cash more checks than manned locations because

the machines can operate 24 hours a day, seven days a week,
Stinson said.

Mr. Payroll owns the software in the machine, Stinson
said. A patent is pending on the operating system. NCR
makes the cashing dispensing part of the machine.

*"And he had power to give life unto the image of the beast,
that the image of the beast should both speak, and cause that
as many as would not worship the image of the beast should
be killed.*

*"And he causeth all, both small and great, rich and poor,
free and bond, to receive a mark in their right hand, or in
their foreheads:*

*"And that no man might buy or sell, save he that had the
mark, or the name of the beast, or the number of his name"*
(Revelation 13:15–17).

This automated check-cashing scheme is surely preparing
us for the ultimate electronic activities involving the mark,
the number and the image of the Beast!

Another article in *Dave Webber Reports*, November
1996, shows how robots will take the entertainment world
by storm. Eventually the world won't even be excited about
performing robots. My good friend Dr. David Breese, sent
me an amazing article that describes an amazing robot that
looks like a teenage girl who sings and speaks several languages. But it's really a robot created by science and computer wizardry. The Bible tells us about such things.

I'm quoting *Popular Science*, August 1996. The following article was by Belinda Luscombe:

Does Brandy Know About This?

In a country that likes its teen singing stars mass-produced,
Kyoko Date is unique. The perky Japanese teenager sings,
speaks several languages and works 24 hours a day. Months

before her debut, she was besieged with requests for interviews and TV appearances. The surge of interest in an unknown talent is unprecedented, says manager Yoshitaka Horl. But Dale isn't superhuman.

In fact, she isn't human at all. A Tokyo talent agency created her, using all the characteristics its departments wanted in a star, plus some computer wizardry. When the computer graphics are finished, she'll release her first CD. Then she'll star in video and computer games. After that, pick your own scandal.

The information super highway is leading us swiftly into the new millennium. There is no turning back. The incredible changes, innovations, perplexities, and amazing inventions will continue in fulfillment of prophecy, especially Daniel 11:4. *"Many shall run to and fro and knowledge shall be increased!"*

Another incredible change that will radically affect our fast-changing world will be driving by computer. We will sit back and relax and a computer will be in the driver's seat. *Dave Webber Reports*, November 1996, (Page 5) reported:

Driving...by Computers!

Driving on our fast freeways becomes more challenging all the time, as traffic increases and speed limits are raised.

Picture traffic that is totally computerized and automated, a highway where technology is in control, not the driver.

I'm quoting an article in *The Washington Times*, dated August 18, 1996, In The Future, the car—and the road—will drive you.

Twenty years from now, falling asleep at the wheel may be a pleasant diversion rather than a quick route to the grave.

Scientists at the University of California at Berkeley and other research centers are trying to take the thrills and danger

out of driving by turning control of your car over to computers in the vehicle or along the road. Automated highway systems promise to double or triple the capacity of today's
congested roads, cut trip times and prevent many of the
40,000 fatalities that now occur each year.

In August, 1997, the California Department of
Transportation (Caltrans) will oversee tests of human-driven
cars with sensors that keep them in their lanes and a safe distance from other vehicles. It also will test a system where
drivers put their cars on auto-pilot. They will be driven on a
car-pool lane on Interstate 15 near San Diego by transmitters
from a control center.

Automatic vehicle control can assist the driver or eliminate him, said William Stevens, technical director of the
National Automated Highway System Consortium, funded
by the Federal Government and industry. The average human
takes half a second or more to react [to conditions on the
road]. Sensors can react in milliseconds.

The consortium members include General Motors,
Hughes Aircraft, Bechtel, Caltrans, the University of
California and Lockheed Martin.

Basic collision avoidance systems for vehicles may be
ready for commercial rollout in just a few years, Mr. Stevens
predicts. Radar or vision-based sensors in the front of your
car will keep it a safe stopping distance from the car ahead.
Other sensors will correct steering to keep your car within its
lane. The National Highway Traffic Safety Administration
estimates such technology could cut crashes by 17%. In a
fully automated system on dedicated lanes or highways,
which might become feasible in 20 years, cars would be controlled by a traffic center and run very close together at high
speeds.

Without people weaving in and out of lanes, slowing
down or speeding up, automated highways could become

much safer and more efficient than today—though drivers
will need a lot of psychological adjustment to hand over
steering to a computer.

Engineers at U.C. Berkeley have developed platoons of
cars that move in tandem only 10 feet apart at 65 miles per
hour. Mr. Stevens admitted he was apprehensive at first
about riding in one. But then you realize it's not scary—it's
like riding in a train, he said. The vehicle in front stays a
constant distance away.

In a recent speech to the World Congress of the
International Federation of Automatic Control (IFAC) in San
Francisco, Mr. Stevens said the stakes are high. The Federal
Government estimates that road congestion costs the nation
$100 billion a year in lost productivity and that road acci-
dents—90% of which are caused by human error—cause
more than 1.7 million disabling injuries a year.

With total vehicle miles traveled expected to double by
2020, Congress in 1991 asked the Department of Transportation to undertake a high-tech program to reduce congestion and accidents, with funding of more than $800 million
over five years.

Beside car-control technology, other systems under development include on-board navigation systems to help drivers
find the best route, automatic road signs to divert traffic
away from congested areas and electronic tolling.

Europe and Japan are hard at work on similar technology.

At the recent IFAC conference, Jurgen Ackermann, director of the Institute of Robotics and System Dynamics near
Munich, won a medal for lifetime contributions to control
technology, including a novel system for preventing cars
from swerving due to icy roads or strong side winds.

Using a cheap gyroscope and an electronic mechanism for
front steering control derived from space robotics research,
the system allowed drivers of a specially-equipped BMW

sedan to stay on course when hitting a slippery patch of a test
track, where even professionals lost control without the system.

Mr. Ackermann said he has talked with BMW and parts
makers such as Bosch about the technology, but has no com-
mitments.

Finally, planners have nightmares about liability issues on
automated highways run by public agencies. A highway system failure could have catastrophic results, noted a
Congressional Budget Office report last year

A flat tire or other breakdown could cause massive dis-
ruption in an automated highway system.

Such an electronic scenario could be a fulfillment of
Nahum's prophecy in Nahum 2:4, *"The chariots shall rage
in the streets, they shall jostle one against another in the
broad ways: they shall seem like torches, they shall run like
the lightnings."*

In recent months, I have seen articles in *The Jerusalem
Report* and *The Jerusalem Post* about the increase of bird
activity in Israel. Huge flying vultures have a natural habi-
tat in Africa, but Israel becomes their natural land corridor
for migration. Today, instead of laying 1 or 2 eggs, it seems
they are laying 3 or 4 eggs and these giant birds are creating safety problems for the Israeli Air Force.

The Coming Composite Beast

*"And I stood upon the sand of the sea, and saw a beast rise
up out of the sea, having seven heads and ten horns, and
upon his head is the name of blasphemy.*

*"And the Beast which I saw was like unto a leopard, and
his feet were as the feet of a bear, and his mouth as the
mouth of a lion: and the dragon gave him his power, and his
seat, and great authority.*

"And I saw one of his heads as it were wounded to death; and his deadly wound was healed: and all the world wondered after the Beast. And they worshipped the dragon which gave power unto the Beast: and they worshipped the Beast, saying, Who is like unto the Beast? Who is able to make war with him?" (Revelation 13:1–4).

This composite beast is the same one viewed in Daniel 7. Only instead of 4 beasts, now there is only one. The characteristics of the Beast kingdoms are merged into one final Gentile empire. The climax of this kingdom is a one-world government! The issue of the mark and number, and numerical value of the Beast's name isn't forced, but it is done!

The one-world concept is being promoted by the United Nations, by NAFTA and by the Common Market! Their goal is to have everything ready by 2000.

"And here is the mind which hath wisdom. The seven heads are seven mountains, on which the woman sitteth.

"And there are seven kings: five are fallen, and one is, and the other is not yet come; and when he cometh, he must continue a short space.

"And the beast that was, and is not, even he is the eighth, and is of the seven, and goeth into perdition.

"And the ten horns which thou sawest are ten kings, which have received no kingdom as yet; but receive power as kings one hour with the beast.

"These have one mind, and shall give their power and strength unto the beast.

"These shall make war with the Lamb, and the Lamb shall overcome them: for he is Lord of lords, and King of kings: and they that are with him are called, and chosen, and faithful.

"And he saith unto me, The waters which thou sawest, where the whore sitteth, are peoples, and multitudes, and nations, and tongues.

"And the ten horns which thou sawest upon the beast, these shall hate the whore, and shall make her desolate and naked, and shall eat her flesh, and burn her with fire.

"For God hath put in their hearts to fulfil his will, and to agree, and give their kingdom unto the beast, until the words of God shall be fulfilled.

"And the woman which thou sawest is that great city, which reigneth over the kings of the earth." (Revelation 17:9−18).

This passage shows the course of Gentile history—politically, religiously, and economically until the end of days.

The final epilogue is given concerning the satanic duo in Revelation 19:19−21.

"And I saw the beast, and the kings of the earth, and their armies, gathered together to make war against him that sat on the horse, and against his army.

"And the beast was taken, and with him the false prophet that wrought miracles before him, with which he deceived them that had received the mark of the beast, and them that worshipped his image. These both were cast alive into a lake of fire burning with brimstone.

"And the remnant were slain with the sword of him that sat upon the horse, which sword proceeded out of his mouth: and all the fowls were filled with their flesh."

The event is Armageddon, the land corridor Israel. God's Son will make an end of all the armies of all nations on this historic battlefield and He will call for the multiplying vultures to cleanse the land of the great slaughter. *"And he hath on his vesture and on his thigh a name written, KING OF KINGS, AND LORD OF LORDS"* (Revelation 19:16). ■

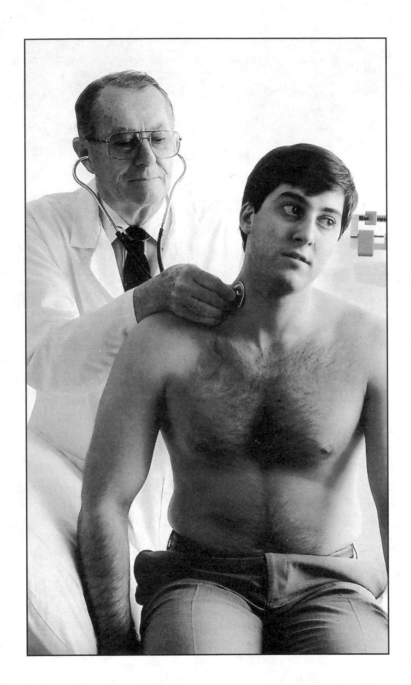

CHAPTER ELEVEN

AIDS Update

—by Dr. John Cionci

Summary

We trace the AIDS epidemic, the worst medical catastrophe to ever hit the world. Dr. Cionci points out that current optimism about this epidemic will give way to new opportunistic infections that will bring unimaginable devastation to the world's populations, especially in the Third World. We show you how AIDS is the gateway to the endtime pestilences described in the Bible. This chapter is sobering yet rooted in the hope of Bible prophecy, which has foretold it all.

There is an evil moving across this land. Slowly and silently, it enters our bodies. This evil has no face except the faces with hollow eyes and sunken cheeks. This evil has no voice except among the dying, and the crying of the infants afflicted.

This evil knows no boundaries at it moves from city to city, state to state, country to country, and finally, continent to continent.

Once inside our bodies, it enters all of our bodily fluids, especially our blood, which is the essence of life itself, and seminal fluid, which is the conveyor of new life.

This evil is spread from person to person primarily by those who indulge in illicit behavior and sometimes it is transmitted from mother to infant—the sins of the parents visited upon the children. Evil begets evil, if you will.

The name of this evil is AIDS (Acquired Immune Deficiency Syndrome), and it will be with us until Jesus returns with His new Kingdom.

In my opinion, AIDS is the disease that most closely fits the endtime scenario because it is sexually transmitted, and we can choose whether or not we wish to risk becoming infected.

Most diseases, such as arthritis, leukemia, and diabetes, have no element of personal moral accountability. But AIDS does. You do have a choice! Praise the Lord!

I was going to write about AIDS and pick out the news highlights about the disease from the past year. But, instead, I'm going to present my theory that AIDS is the *gateway* to the endtime pestilences prophesied in the Bible!

The AIDS virus alone never kills anyone, except when it attacks the brain directly. Rather, it destroys the immune system, allowing other diseases to do the killing.

AIDS appears to be the gateway to endtime pestilences described in the Bible for at least four key reasons.

AIDS: Gateway To Prophesied Endtime Pestilences

Reason#1—AIDS is unique because it is *pandemic.*
Epidemics throughout human history have always had some sort of geographical border, either in a neighbor-hood, a section of a city, an entire city, or a region.

For example, the Black Plague in Europe struck the entire continent. One-third of the people died. But the disease did-n't go beyond that continent. It was an *epidemic* that had a geographical border.

In contrast, AIDS is a *pandemic.* There is no place in the world that this disease has not infected someone. Even Induit indians in the northern-most parts of Canada are infected with it. During the summer months of July and August, the loggers bring it to the women and the disease will probably wipe out the Induits in about one or two decades. Part of the reason the disease has spread quickly among the Induits is that the Induit women, unfortunately, are very naive, and are very free with their bodies. They engage in illicit behavior with the loggers, thus spreading it to the Eskimos.

Reason#2—The antibodies which our immune system produces to fight the AIDS virus are powerless against it.

We have an immune system which consists of white cells to protect us when a virus, bacterium, fungus, or parasite enters our body. A white cell called a "macrophage" goes through the body looking for foreign invaders. If it sees any, it signals the TA cells, also known as CD4 cells. The CD4 cells come, observe, start to replicate themselves, and send chemical impulses to the B-cells, which come and produce antibodies to fight the invader.

In a few hours, a few days, maybe even a few weeks, the disease is conquered and the body is well again. In some cases, we get a bonus—lifetime immunity against that par-ticular disease.

Why is AIDS so different? When AIDS enters our body, the first thing it does is look for our immune system. It looks for the first line of defense: the T4 cells. But the AIDS virus is asexual; it can't reproduce itself! It needs to find a *host*, specifically the CD4 cell. It enters the CD4 cell using an enzyme called "reverse transcriptase." Only then is it empowered to produce another AIDS virus.

But the CD4 cell has been fooled into assuming this newly-replicated AIDS virus is its own cell, so it pops it out into the blood stream. Instead of it being another CD4 cell, it is another AIDS virus. This happens hundreds of times in the same cell. It can happen slowly: reproduce, pop out; reproduce, pop out.

Or the AIDS virus can continue to reproduce while inside the CD4 cell until finally, hundreds, maybe even a thousand viruses exist in one CD4 cell—and it bursts like a pod!

That, in turn, causes a *thousand* new viruses to be pumped throughout the body in the bloodstream, looking for more CD4 cells.

Or the virus can stay inside the cell nucleus of the CD4 cells and become more or less latent.

This is a very insidious disease!

Reason#3—The AIDS virus is continuously *mutating*. In changing one *molecule* of its biological structure, any medication introduced to slow down or kill the AIDS virus is rendered obsolete. This disease is the first one I am aware of that is so unique and unbelievable that it can't be eradicated by the medical science available to us at this time.

Reason#4—Again, the virus itself doesn't cause death, except when it gets to the brain and destroys it. I've been following AIDS since 1985, before actor Rock Hudson died, and at that time we knew very little about it.

I became interested in the disease because I had a part-time position in the Philadelphia Department of Health, where we treated nothing but sexually transmitted diseases. We were force-fed information about HIV and AIDS. In fact, it wasn't even called HIV then; it was called LAV or HTLV3. We didn't even know how it was transmitted!

The clinic did a special secret study for the CDC (Centers For Disease Control) in 1986, and we found out that 7.4% of those coming through our door for syphilis, gonorrhea, and other sexually transmitted diseases were HIV-positive.

Because of the uncertainty about this disease, we were told to wash our hands in household bleach after seeing each patient. The city, to save money, used the cheapest they could buy, and it also had the strongest smell.

It was so bad that when I went home, I entered by the front door and my wife, who was in the back of the house, in the kitchen, could *smell* me before she could *hear* me— that's strong bleach!

The AIDS virus, of course, has no vaccine and no cure. Therefore, it was interesting that President Bill Clinton said,

> In a decade, or within ten years, I believe, we are going to have a vaccine.

Everybody seems to want a *vaccine* more than a *cure*, believe it or not. They want to "have their cake and eat it too," if you follow what I mean. So, people want a vaccine, but how are we going to develop a vaccine to prevent a disease that is continually changing and rechanging inside the same body?

We thought, at one time, that it would be nice if all people who are HIV-positive, all the HIV-positive men and all the HIV-positive women, would form a club—HIV-positive members only—and they could cohabit with each other and they wouldn't harm anyone, because they already had HIV.

Wrong! The strain from the female was different from the strain of the male. They would co-cohabit, and they would now each have two different strains within the same body. They were *accelerating* the chances of dying much sooner than if they just had one strain. So it doesn't work. It's not that easy!

Opportunistic Infections

For HIV-positive patients, a growing list of diseases are called "opportunistic" infections. Normally, they are very commonplace and never really dangerous if you have a normal immune system that is functioning well.

But, in people with HIV and AIDS, with the immune system being eroded and finally being destroyed, these commonplace diseases are life threatening.

Thrush. Very simple and common is a disease called "thrush," which frequently affects babies. In fact, my six-week-old grandson had a mild case. Usually, the disease is not life-threatening and it can often be treated in one day.

But for HIV-positive people, with a compromised immune system, thrush, which is a form of a fungus, can grow so freely in the esophagus that it actually blocks the passage of food into the stomach. Amazing!

In fact, I saw a slide of someone with esophageal thrush who had an opening about a quarter of an inch in diameter. Only fluid could pass through into the stomach.

Oddly, the thrush didn't start in the mouth as usual. For some reason, it bypassed the mouth and started in the esophagus—a very unusual case.

PCP. A disease known as "PCP" is not even a virus or bacterium; it's a *parasite* that grows quickly and afflicts the lungs. On the first day, a patient complaining about a dry hacking cough will be x-rayed. The x-ray may be perfectly normal. Yet an x-ray made three or four days later might indicate that the lungs have suddenly become congested with this parasitic infection known as "pneumocystis." The parasite leaves no air sacs open, no room for air to get in, so patients must be kept alive on a respirator.

This is a life-threatening disease, which I've probably treated in the course of my years in practice.

In 1950, if a person came to my office with a dry hacking cough, I'd listen to his chest. I wouldn't hear too much. The patient would have a low fever, maybe 99 degrees, and I'd prescribe a cough medicine with a suppressant, and antibiotics.

Four days later, the patient would return completely cured. I looked good. It may have been PCP; I have no way of knowing.

We know that PCP is out there, but the immune system of those who are HIV-positive is impaired, making this the #1 killer of people with HIV and AIDS.

KS. Kaposi's Sarcoma is a skin cancer that has been around at least since the late 1800s when it was discovered by a doctor named Kaposi. On white skin it is purplish. On black skin it's darker than the surrounding skin. How can a skin cancer kill you? Well, it can't. Skin cancers don't kill people.

I never saw a Kaposi's Sarcoma the entire time I was in practice until I started to take care of AIDS patients in 1985. Then I began seeing KS often.

KS kills AIDS patients because they have no effective immune system. The skin cancer it enters the body and goes into the liver, kidneys, and other organs. And do you know what happens when you have cancer of the liver? You die. So because of AIDS, we now have a skin cancer that is killing people through destruction of other organs.

The significance of this is that KS is found mostly in gay men. Women and intravenous drug users rarely get KS.

Toxo Plasmosis. This parasite is found in uncooked meat and housecats. Therefore, people with HIV are not allowed to have cats.

One gay man I became acquainted with at the clinic loved his cat so much that he bought a leash and small collar, and trained the cat to go outdoors like a dog with him on a walk.

But otherwise, he was never allowed to change the kitty litter because the oocysts of the toxo plasmosis were in the feces. Moving the litter around might cause him to inhale the toxo plasmosis, which could go into his body and eventually get up to his brain.

Though this has nothing to do with AIDS, pregnant females should also avoid changing kitty litter because even though they are immune to the toxo plasmosis because they have a normal immune system, their unborn infant has an underdeveloped immune system and can be born with toxic plasmosis.

Therefore, pregnant women shouldn't change kitty litter, and they should also cook their meat very well.

Candidiasis, a yeast infection, becomes so overwhelming in female vaginas that it's almost diagnostic for HIV. If it can't be eradicated with a normal antifungal medication, it becomes almost self-diagnostic.

Cervical cancer also becomes a frequent diagnosis for women with HIV. They may be found to have primary cervical cancer before they have any other symptoms, and they don't know it until they do a test to screen for hincryptosporidiosis, a small germ which gets into drinking water.

In Milwaukee, 100,000 people developed diarrhea and abdominal cramps. People with HIV became very ill and some died. Their weakened immune systems couldn't fight off the illness.

I mention these diseases because some of them may be the diseases we read about in the Book of Revelation.

I would like to go into a little more detail with an article that I wrote for the October 1997 issue of *Free Press*. A letter was sent to me from England and the article was about someone who lived in California.

After a year-long search, doctors in California announced the discovery of a previously unknown parasitic worm in a person infected with AIDS who died. After many months of puzzling over the circumstances of the victim's death, scientists employed Polymer Chain Reaction (PCR), a technique used to examine microscopic tissues of organic matter to create millions of copies of some particular useful sequence of DNA from the suspected microbe.

The doctors, to their amazement, found that the large mass of tissue in the abdomen of the patient was scar tissue caused by the rapid growth of this never-before-seen worm.

Now doesn't this sound like a plot out of a Stephen King novel—an internal alien? (Some enterprising author will pick up on this!) I'm always fascinated when life imitates fiction. The worm seems to have a molecular biology resembling that of a tape worm, but of an unknown type or origin, and far more aggressive and ferocious than previously known worms.

Scary, huh? The scientists told reporters they didn't know how often the new worm caused diseases in humans and whether the weakened immune system of a person with AIDS would be a factor in susceptibility, or in the damage caused by this mysterious worm. Nor did the baffled scientists know whether the parasite exists in nature and whether the worm infestation can be treated with drugs known to be effective against similar parasites.

The San Francisco Bay area victim who acquired HIV six years earlier began to experience abdominal and back pain, weight loss, night sweats, and fever in 1994, and was admitted to a hospital in March of 1996.

According to reports, he had never traveled outside the United States, but he was an avid camper. The worm had destroyed parts of his liver and intestine, and doctors have yet to give it a name.

Imagine having a worm eat your internal organs while you are still alive! This is unlike other parasites which *feed* off their hosts, but this one seems intent on *devouring* its host!

Could this be another endtime pestilence, or is it merely a new and exotic disease which eerily seems to only attack people with AIDS? Time will tell, and we seem to be running our of that. Still, the sick need our prayers.

Another article I've written tells of babies in an intensive care unit at a Boston hospital who are being killed by a new strain of a common bug called Pseudomonas Aeruginosa.

The hospital closed the unit to new patients to isolate and identify the deadly bacteria. Officials said the bacteria were found on the hands of several hospital employees.

That is very upsetting to me because those workers could have transmitted this bug to other people in the hospital with weak immune systems: people with HIV and AIDS, those just coming out of surgery, and those having taken radiation or chemotherapy.

Pseudomonas Aeruginosa — Endtime Sores?

I have heard about, and seen slides of dermatological manifestations of Pseudomonas Aeruginosa. It brings to mind prophetic passages in the Bible about sores on the body in the endtimes.

When this Pseudomonas attacks AIDS patients, they develop chronic leg ulcers, macerated toe webs, buttocks lesions requiring wide incisions, and bacteremia, a condition in which there is so much bacteria in the blood that the patient is overwhelmed. It's like blood poisoning caused by bacteria. As bad as this sounds, if treated early with certain antibiotics, it can be cured. But, if this is a new strain, that may not be possible.

People often pick up Pseudomonas from vegetables and fruit. It's very commonplace but rarely do those who are exposed become very sick. Frighteningly, but interestingly, Pseudomonas Aeruginosa infections occur most often in *hospitals*, where the organism is frequently found in moist areas such as basins, antiseptic solutions, and urine receptacles.

Hold on. Did you say "antiseptic solutions"? You mean if a nurse inserting an IV [intra-venous needle] in a patient has used an antiseptic contaminated by Pseudomonas, then the bacteria can go directly into the patient's bloodstream and kill him? I sure hope I don't need an IV the next time I go to the hospital! Pseudomonas Aeruginosa infects thousands of critically ill patients every year, and it's especially dangerous to premature babies, probably because of their underdeveloped immune systems.

Having said all this, I will now make a prediction: If this is, in fact, a new strain of Pseudomonas Aeruginosa, and it is resistant to antibiotics, then it will be added to the growing list of opportunistic infections that viciously attack people with HIV and AIDS. Are these the endtimes, or what?

Now, I want to discuss three diseases with you. One is old, one is rather new, and one is both old and new.

The first, the old one, is leprosy. The bacterium is called Myco-Bacterium Leprae.

The second one, the new one, is called Myco-Bacterium Avium Complex.

The third one, which is both old and new, is called Myco-Bacterium Tuberculosis.

Now, as you see, the commonality is the genus: They are all myco-bacteria. Myco-bacteria have a waxy substance around their outer covering, making them impervious to a lot of medications. They are well protected and it takes more than one medication to attack them. You can't attack them with just one drug. You have to use at least *four*.

The Myco-Bacterium Leprae has been around since ancient times, and it's more or less endemic. We find it in Southeast Asia, maybe some parts of southern China, but it's really not that prevalent.

Now, let's talk about Myco-Bacterium Avium Complex (MAC). Before the AIDS pandemic, disseminated infection with the MAC organism was extremely uncommon. The first reports of the disease were in 1982.

Since then, it has been widely recognized as an opportunistic pathogen infecting at least 20% of AIDS patients. "Avium" means the avian type commonly produces disease in chickens and swine, and only rarely infected humans until AIDS came along.

Thirdly, we'll discuss Myco-Bacterium Tuberculosis.

When I first went into practice, people who worked in a beauty salon, barber shop or restaurant would have to go to the doctor to get a referral for a chest X-ray at our health center which offered free chest x-rays for these workers.

These workers would return with the negative report, and the doctor would fill out a form allowing them to work for another year. Because this was done every year, tuberculosis declined to the point that it was almost eradicated.

Tuberculosis was going down until 1985 (AIDS started in 1981) when it leveled off. Then in 1986, it started to go up. TB was making a comeback. Astounding! It was making a comeback in people with HIV and AIDS!

Everyone is carrying a tubercle bacillus in his or her body. Everyone has been exposed to the coughing and sneezing of others, but our immune system protects us from tuberculosis, and builds up resistance so we can't be overcome by it. If you do happen to become susceptible, there are medications which will cure you.

The people with HIV were normal until their immune system started to go down. That allowed the TB in their body a chance to emerge. The frightening part of it is that it came back with a vengeance. People were put on the four drugs, which you must take if you are HIV-positive, for at least 1.5—2 years, maybe for life.

Patients are not going to live that long anyway when they are in the final stages of AIDS. Patients who are HIV-positive in the early stages may be taking them for at least 10–12 years.

Now, let me trace the tragic path of this disease. If a patient's coughing stops, and he or she is no longer expectorating blood into a tissue, the patient may forget to take the medication.

In other cases, the patient may not feel like taking the medication, may be high on drugs or drunk, or may be trading sex for crack cocaine at a "crack house." The salient factor is that patients who don't take their TB medicine suffer the catastrophic results which, by the way, endanger others.

Tuberculosis bacilli that have been given a punch and knocked down, but not out (completely killed), get up off the floor and become bigger and stronger than ever! This newly strengthened, energized and deadly disease, MDRTB (Multiple Drug Resistant Tuberculosis) is now on the loose.

This is scary because I can contract MDRTB from a patient and die in about 4 weeks. Knowing that tuberculosis is making this strong comeback, and MAC is killing people with HIV, another part of my theory is that *leprosy* is going to be added to the list of opportunistic infections in those parts of the world where it is endemic.

If you have a disease that a few hundred people have, and you're living in over-congested conditions as are those in most poor countries, it's only a matter of time before this spreads. The people with HIV are the ones who are going to contract it first.

But the frightening aspect is that HIV is so unique. People with HIV in their body have no immune system, and the only thing they have to fight diseases with are the drugs.

So doctors prescribe drugs. But, to combat a disease properly, a patient must have an immune system as well as drugs in order to *recover*. You see, people with no resistance can only rely on drugs. If the drugs don't kill all of the disease, every last one of those germs, *then the patient is a breeding ground for a virulent superbug that becomes increasingly difficult to contain*.

Now, my theory becomes even scarier! Hold on to yourself as you read this: People with HIV are *incubators* for super germs. Does that sound crazy? I don't think it's crazy at all, but if I said this to the medical society, they'd take away my license and I'd probably get bashed on the radio and everywhere else. But that's OK. That's just my hunch of what might be happening in these endtimes.

We'll never know, because we'll be in heaven. A news clipping stated:

> "Drug resistant TB threatens health crisis. Our world again faces the spector of incurable tuberculosis. Hot zones of untreatable tuberculosis are emerging around the world and threatening a global crisis," the World Health Organization said. A study of 50,000 patients in 35 nations found that a third of the countries have a form of TB resistant to multiple drugs. Untreatable cases account for 2–14% of the world's total.

That doesn't sound like much, but considering the population of the world, it's a lot of people. WHO (World Health

Organization) said lethal tuberculosis could spread rapidly because only one in ten patients get medical care appropriate to curb drug resistance.

In other words, unless someone has a health care worker handing him the pills every single morning, watching him put them in his mouth, watching him swallow them with some water, how do you know if he took those pills?

Who mainly has tuberculosis? People in crowded neighborhoods, the homeless, the drug addicted, the alcoholics, the women on crack cocaine who exchange sex for drugs. These are the ones who are going to get this disease. They in turn will infect others with whom they come in contact.

Hot zones for TB in India? That figures, as well as in Russia, Latvia, the Dominican Republic, Argentina, and the Ivory Coast. It's already in three different continents. According to the study by the World Health Organization and U.S. officials, patients threaten to overwhelm local health systems.

The study shows definitively, and for the first time, that possibility which we have most feared but couldn't previously prove.

"Our world *again* faces the spector of *incurable* tuberculosis," said Dr. Michael Iceman, TB Chief at the National Jewish Medical and Research Center in Denver.

Tuberculosis, the world's leading infectious killer, is spread through coughing and sneezing, singing, yelling, even talking. The average patient infects 10–20 people a year!

The disease often can be cured with a combination of four drugs taken for 6–12 months. But many patients, especially in poor countries, stop taking the drugs when they feel better or run out of money. This allows the TB still in their bodies to rebound and then the situation is worse: They have created a disease with increasing drug resistance!

These people can also spread the drug-resistant TB to new patients, a circumstance that gives patients a condition that is called "*primary* drug resistance."

In other words, image this scenario: Someone is going to the hospital for an accident. He has a cough and is put into a surgical ward. He coughs in the room. The air conditioning intake sucks up the aerosolized droplets of his cough. This is how tuberculosis is spread.

Just suppose that the droplets are carried into the ventilation system and they go to other people on the floor who are weakened. They may have just had surgery, or chemotherapy or maybe a transplant that has left their immune system down. It's very possible that those people might come down with MDRTB.

This very incident happened in 1994 in New York City in one of the biggest hospitals in the country. Six people died of MDRTB, because the ventilating system transmitted the infection from one patient. More got sick, but they didn't all die.

That's why—when I say that leprosy may become another opportunistic infection walking through the door opened by the AIDS virus—I don't think I'm basing my opinion on anything other than sound logic and reasoning based on a clinical understanding of how diseases develop, mutate, and spread. When I consider the possibilities for an uncontrollable outbreak of dangerous diseases, and while praying for mercy on all of humanity, I sincerely hope that I am wrong!　■

CHAPTER TWELVE

2,000 A.D. Are You Ready?

—by Peter Lalonde

Summary

Even if the Lord doesn't return in the next few years, we're in for a change anyway—not as dramatic, but almost as dramatic. Take a front row seat with us as we take a journey with one of the world's most forward-thinking Bible prophecy analysts.

My subject is *2000 A.D.—Are You Ready?*, which also happens to be the title of a book I wrote with my brother Paul. We chose it very carefully. We wanted it to be a provocative question for Christians and for non-Christians. *Are you ready?* Ready for what? What do people think the year 2000 is going to mean?

Many have done complex calculations and have come up with the year 2000 as being a very prophetic date, perhaps for the Lord's return. They have done the calculations based on the six days and on the 6,000 years, and so on and so forth. On one hand, you could say it's crazy. If the Lord wanted us to know the day of His return, He'd have given us the exact dates from which to calculate it.

On the other hand, you could say, "Look at the way God provided the dates for the Lord's first coming. Would He not give us the same provision for the Second Coming if He wanted us to have it?"

The Rapture and the Second Coming are two separate events. People often get confused about this and consider them to be the same event. They then proceed to try to calculate the date of the Rapture of the church.

Let's forget the calculations. We can simply look at all the signs of the times and prophecies and say, "It looks pretty close."

All these fulfillments are happening as we approach the year 2000. So you have to sit back and say, "Well, maybe we can't calculate something from it, but maybe, on the other hand, we should, as Christians, be expecting our Lord to return soon." Not just because of the year 2000, but because of all the signs of the times that are being fulfilled.

The year 2000 gets a lot of people interested in prophecy, which could in turn lead them to the Lord. Therefore, we must use prophecy as a witnessing tool without being sensational about it or about the year 2000.

Let's talk about the secular world now. We make a provocative statement in *2000 A.D.—Are Your Ready?*:

> If the Lord does return in the next few years, this world is going to change quite a lot. Do we agree? The Tribulation Period begins. Seven years later, the Lord returns for the Second Coming to set up His millennial kingdom. We are talking about some pretty massive changes here on Earth.

But I will also say this: Even if the Lord doesn't return in the next few years, we're in for a change anyway—not as dramatic, but almost as dramatic.

You see, (now I will have to count myself as part of the "older generation") when I started talking to my nephew not so long ago, I realized that we didn't really have a clue what the other was talking about. We just sat there looking at each other for a minute and realized the different worlds in which we live.

But in our generation, that's yours and mine, and I'm dividing the line at about age 35 now, it's sort of business as usual out there, right? The world is changing, things are happening, but we're going with the flow. We're just in a bit of a transition period. I don't think many people realize this, once again, because of the different generations.

The younger generation—and my brother Paul and I do sort of sit on the borderline of this—is living in a world that many don't even know exists. They're living in a world of virtual reality, the Internet, cyberspace, megabytes, ram, and Pentium processors. Many people in our generation don't know the meaning of those words. Not for all of them, but for the large majority, these words are not a part of the everyday vocabulary for the over-35 population. If you want to know which side of the generation gap you're on, think about your VCR. Is it still flashing on midnight?

Come on. Tell the truth. Now have your grandson over. In ten seconds he will have the thing getting channels you didn't even know existed and he'll have the clock going. This is his world.

The younger generation sees changes coming that many barely comprehend.

What's special about the year 2000? What's its significance, prophetically? I don't think you can calculate anything on a date. But let's say the Lord doesn't return before 2000. We better look about because we'll have to go public with our ministries and bail out because business will be done.

Furthermore, we'll be preaching only to a few at that point in time. I think many would agree with that. People go with the wave, and when the wave is gone, look out.

The year 2000 is significant in the fact that it is a metaphor. For many Christians, it has come to mean the possible return of the Lord.

For the world, it means all of this prophecy and end-of-the-world foolishness will finally be put to rest so that mankind can take the next step into the future. Two completely different world views meet up at the year 2000, and a conflict is emerging. If you are reading the secular literature today, you can clearly see this conflict approaching.

Those who are looking for the expansion of human potential and the future of the universe, the *Star Trek* generation, and so on, see the year 2000 as a new beginning. Our beliefs, those of us who believe in the literal message of Bible prophecy, are seen as the outmoded ones that will fade away after the year 2000.

Have you heard of the famous radio program and the book, "War of the Worlds"? The book was released in 1898 and that's why it became a big deal. It wasn't because it was about Martians. *It was because it drove the world crazy as it approached the next century.* Isn't it interesting that many today are interested in aliens and extra-terrestrials as we face another turn of the century into a new millennium?

Now, we've got to agree that the year 1900 was nowhere near as significant as the year 2000 as we watch all the images and ideas coming upon the world today.

In our book, *2000 A.D.—Are You Ready?* we look at how the world is changing. Not how events are changing, but how we as human beings are changing.

I believe we are completely different from any generation that has come before us. Harrod's Department store in London, around the year 1900, installed a new device that totally flipped the people out. It was called an *escalator*! It took people up from the first floor to the second floor. Nobody would get on the thing. They were afraid of it.

They were saying things like, "Do you not realize what will happen to our brains with the sudden rise in altitude?" Harrod's served people a glass of brandy at the top of the escalator to help them get over the "change in altitude."

I think my great-grandfather just kept going around and around. Just kidding. People were horrified. That was one hundred years ago.

What about today? How do we accept change today? Is this not a society that is defined by the saying "Been there, done that"? Give us something new.

When some of us were younger, Buck Rogers would come on the air. We wondered if Buck Rogers' world could happen in our lifetime.

Today, in a world where there is virtual reality, cloning, *Jurassic Park* and *ET*, kids wonder if the new thing will be out by Christmas. Their expectations are different. Did you know that the number-one complaint by kids today is "boredom"? They are bored silly. Can you imagine putting some of these kids on a farm?

Indeed, it is a world that has changed much, and that is *expecting* much change. If something new doesn't come along, well....

My young niece might play with a new toy for a few minutes, and then she will happily play with a cardboard box or coasters for the rest of the day. But as kids get older, they'll play with something for five minutes and then wonder what's next. If you're trying to keep your kids or grandkids supplied with video games, you know what it's costing you.

Many of us don't even know how the technology works, but we want it anyway.

One Saturday morning the phone rang about 8 a.m. I was planning to sleep in because I had worked late the night before.

My brother was calling to say he had a terrible incident at his house. During the night the batteries on his TV clicker had died. He didn't know what to do so he called to ask me to turn on my TV and flip through the channels so I could tell him what was on. That way he'd only have to get up to change the channel once and he wouldn't have to stand there waiting through a commercial to find out what was on. The idea of getting up every time he wanted to change the channel seemed remote, pardon the pun.

It's a new world of expectations today. We expect everything to be readily at our fingertips. Yet we don't know how everything works. We turn on a light switch, but we don't really know how it works. We know our VCRs can record a TV program in the middle of the night, but we don't know how. We just accept these things as part of our world. And not only that, we expect things to get bigger, better and faster very, very quickly.

Things are happening so fast that we have two generations in one period of history today. Using the age of 35 as our borderline once again, we have an over-35 generation which is very much *out of touch* with the under-35 generation.

Many didn't get a computer when they were first becoming popular and now they just look at the things and scratch their heads. Let me sidetrack for a moment here. You're not going to have to know much about computers in the future.

Let's say you want to record our *This Week in Bible Prophecy* program Thursday night at 7:30 on TBN. You have to find a blank video tape and you have to remember to program your VCR to record the show. Now, you've decided to tape the program, but you notice your time on the VCR is flashing at midnight. Now you have to figure out, first of all, how to set the time on the VCR. Then, when you get that working, you have to figure out how to program your VCR to know which Thursday you're talking about and what channel you want to record. It's an enormous pain.

And how about that special on Israel on A&E on Tuesday night at 8 that you didn't even know about? You're missing programs that you would really like to see because you didn't even know they were on!

In the future, however, you will be able to walk up to your VCR and simply *say*, "This Week in Bible Prophecy." The VCR will record the program every time it's on. You won't have to do a lot of programming for that.

Indeed, technology is getting that smart. What do I mean by "smart"? Well, let's say you tell your VCR to record "This Week in Bible Prophecy" and Zola Levitt's program as well as Jack Van Impe's. The VCR will take the liberty to record Dave Breese's program as well, because it has learned what you like to watch. We're only a couple of years away from this type of technology.

You will wake up in the morning a few years from now to the aroma of brewed coffee because the machine knows what time you get up. You'll be awakened by the news on

the radio. But it won't be the same news your neighbor will
be hearing because your radio will know the kind of news
you're interested in. The broadcast will be personalized just
for you.

You will get into your shower, which will happen to
already be running. Your clothes will have been selected
based on the day's weather forecast. Your phone will ring
and when you answer it, a message will say you weren't
awakened with a phone call at 5:30 in the morning because
it was only your brother Paul calling about his TV remote
again. The message will also tell you that your car is low on
gas so you better stop and fill up on the way to the office
because you won't have enough to make it there. You'll also
be told that the traffic going east will be heavy this morning, so you should consider going to the ESSO station to
your west. This is all just a few years away.

I believe the Lord has called Paul and me for the exact
moment because we are right at that middle age where we
are half in that world. We watch Star Trek and we're on the
Internet. We enjoy all these things. On the other hand, we're
old enough that the younger generation is way ahead of us.

One time, Paul and I were at the computer store looking
for a new monitor. We were thinking about its speed, and
whether it displayed good graphics, mainly so we could play
really cool games.

Two kids, about ten years old, were standing near us.
Hearing them talk about computers made us realize that they
were technologically far ahead of us. We felt like dinosaurs.
We didn't have a clue what they were talking about and
when we asked them for advice, they just looked at us like
we were a couple of idiots. Because of this "generation
gap," many kids have no respect for adults today. Change is
happening so quickly that most in the older generation can't
keep up with the younger population.

Think of the prophecy in Daniel, chapter 12 that says in the endtimes, knowledge shall be increased. Name another generation that fits this prophecy. Of course, knowledge has increased in every generation. But either Daniel was saying nothing, because this prophecy fits any generation, or he was saying something about a *unique* generation. I think he was saying something about the generation unique to—that is, parallel to—the Lord's return.

This prophecy can't fit any past generation. Let's say you had a time travel machine and you could go back to the year 400. You're on a ship sailing around the world. Then you tell the time travel machine to take you to the year 1800 and you end up on a ship again. Is it not pretty much the same ship? Then you tell the machine to take you to the year 1997 and suddenly you're on an airplane landing in the middle of a runway at DFW airport.

Previously, you could go from generation to generation without seeing many major changes. But when you come to this generation, you could drop dead of a heart attack from the shock of all the changes you would see. Planes are flying overhead. There are the Internet, computers, television. My parents actually didn't have television or refrigerators. They had an outhouse. It's incredible to me. But it's all happened in this very generation, that quickly.

I'll tell you a story. I don't know where I get this great stuff, but, here goes. A father has two sons. The older son is very bright and a bit taller than his brother. The younger son isn't so bright. He's got a beard and he's eleven years old. These two hypothetical brothers are given a choice by their father. He tells them he'll pay their allowance for the whole year in the month of January.

"I'll give you one thousand dollars" (he's doing well, apparently), he says, "or I'll give you a penny on the first day of January, two pennies on the second day, four pennies on the third day, eight pennies on the fourth day, and so on. I'll just double that penny."

Well, the younger brother with the beard jumps right on the thousand bucks. He says, "Yup, I'm sold."

Now let's do some calculating. At the end of the first week the younger brother had his thousand bucks. The older brother had $1.27. He's one week into the month and not doing so well.

At the end of the second week, the younger brother still has his thousand bucks and the older brother has $163. He's still getting killed. The younger brother has bought a new bike.

By the end of the third week, however, the older, smarter brother has $20,971.51, just from doubling those pennies everyday. All the younger brother has is his bike and the change left over from a thousand bucks.

But we're only three weeks in. At the end of the fourth week, the 28th of January, the older brother now has $2,684,354.55. There's still three days left in January.

On the 29th of January, there is $5,300,000 and change.

On the 30th, there's $10,737,000 and change.

And on the 31st, there's $21,474,000, just by doubling up pennies for 30 days.

This is the power of exponential growth. And this is similar to how knowledge is increasing today. A lot of articles are saying now that the estimates are that human knowledge is doubling from anywhere from two to four years. Computer technology is doubling every eighteen months.

This means that everything mankind learned from the time of Adam to 1995 was half of what we know today. And everything we learned from 1995 until now is the other half of what we know. We always hear the story that we've gone from the Wright brothers to the space shuttle in one lifetime. And we have.

The question we have to ask now is "Where are we going from the space shuttle and how quickly?" I say all of that to say that we started out by talking about expectations. Think of what we have seen in our lifetime and what our kids have seen in theirs. Where will we be a few years from now? Would you not like to say, and here's a statement I'd be afraid to make, "It'll never happen!" You could look like a moron pretty quickly in our world today.

Here's a case in point: When the movie *Jurassic Park* came out, people were amazed. The movie was about finding a mosquito that had bitten a dinosaur, drank its blood and then got encased in amber so that it was perfectly preserved for thousands of years.

Then, in modern times, the fly was discovered, the DNA from the dinosaur's blood was extracted and a dinosaur was recreated.

We interviewed some people afterwards for *This Week in Bible Prophecy* and people were saying they were wishing we could find a fly with dinosaur blood and recreate a dinosaur today.

We were amused by these people, thinking, "The issue isn't whether you can find a fly with dinosaur DNA, but whether you could recreate a dinosaur using the DNA."

Then, not long afterward, the report came out about Dolly, the sheep that was cloned in Scotland. Indeed, how close are we to things that may seem incredible today? But people believe that, maybe in just five years, we can see this or that happen because we've seen so much *already* in our lifetime.

When something amazing happens in our world, it is easy to sometimes take it in stride because we *expect* it.

In 1976, Paul and I went to see the movie, *Indiana Jones: Raiders of the Lost Ark*. When we came out of the movie we'd find pieces of rope and things like that and crack them like whips at each other, just like when the kids came out of the Karate Kid movies and kicked garbage cans over all the way home.

Anyway, Paul and I were walking along the lake shore back to our house, wrestling and trying to decide who was going to be Indiana Jones and who was going to be the bad guy.

It was dark out and we saw a light shining on the surface of the water. We went closer to the water's edge to take a look because it seemed a little strange. The light was dancing over the surface of the water. We looked up for a street light. There was none.

We looked for the moon. It was an overcast night, as dark as can be. We were wondering where the light was coming from. I suggested we explore. Paul was a little frightened, so I started walking into the water, fully clothed, at 11 at night.

If this was a secret passageway to another dimension or a mystery, well, I was Indiana Jones, and I was going to discover it. We walked out to the light, getting closer and closer, with Paul right behind me, and I reached out my toe to touch the light. The light started to spin around under the surface. Well, the adventure of the "Indiana Lalondes," it turns out, was to discover a flashlight in the lake. Some thief being chased by the police threw the light into the lake. He had burglarized a house nearby.

Instead, if we had been coming home from a baseball game that night, would we have gone into the water after the light? Probably not. But we were coming home from an Indiana Jones movie and we had a set of expectations, a set of beliefs that were fully operational in our minds.

Now, let me ask you a different question. If we had been coming home from the movie *Jaws*, how many millions of dollars would it have taken for us to walk into that lake in the dark?

My wife was uncomfortable about swimming in anything other than a pool for years after seeing *Jaws*. Think about the context that much of the world has today to draw its expectations from—the big screen. This is the perspective that our world has today.

When you go to the movies and see Arnold Swartzenegger jump off a ten-story building and then get up and keep chasing a bad guy, you actually believe he did that. If he did this in real life, he'd be dead. But in the movies, it looks real. It took 20 stunt men and 30 days of shooting, with a whole bunch of beanbags for these guys to land on, to create this sequence. But when you watch it, you are convinced that these kinds of impossible feats are *possible*.

What would happen, now that the world has seen *ET* and *Independence Day* on the big screen, if suddenly we were to hear that contact with alien beings has been made? Isn't everyone going to immediately believe it's *possible* because they've seen it in a Hollywood movie?

Let me tell you about two displays at the Smithsonian Institute that deal with space flight: The Apollo 11 Command Capsule is one. Across the hall is a model of *The Starship Enterprise*. That Apollo 11 capsule has actually been to the moon. The Starship Enterprise is made of plastic and has never gone anywhere, except over the the airwaves. Which one do you think gets more visitors? For every person who visits the Apollo 11 display, ten visit The Starship Enterprise display. It's about *expectations*.

I remember when my cousin had a seance with some friends when they were kids. They went down to the basement and put curtains over the windows.

They were sitting around a table with a burning candle on it, and they decided to call back Martin Luther King who had recently been shot. They asked that he come back in a strange form. Just as they did, a spider dropped down from the ceiling, right in the middle of them. Well, they all went screaming upstairs, crying, because they were convinced they had turned Martin Luther King into a spider!

Now it doesn't matter that they didn't. What does matter is that they were *expecting* it because they *believed* it was going to happen. When something did happen, they *interpreted* it to be what they were *expecting*.

So, if the whole world is expecting something big to happen as we approach the year 2000, isn't everything that takes place going to be amplified?

Let's say Saddam Hussein had invaded Kuwait in 1999 instead of 1990. Would this situation have been read much differently? Would more people have thought that the Battle of Armageddon was not far off and that the end of the world was coming?

Watch the next couple of years. When people want something to happen badly enough, they are going to find a way to make it happen.

I mentioned that the possibility of alien contact is more believable than ever today.

When pictures of the universe were coming back from the Hubble Space Telescope, many were thinking that they had no idea how staggering the universe really is, and that maybe there has to be life out there.

Let's say the year is 1865 again and Clint Eastwood and Dave Breese are having a gunfight. A UFO lands and they both have a heart attack because they have no context whatsoever to deal with this metal ship landing on Earth. But if a UFO were to land in our generation, the next thing we might see is a Larry King special interview with ET.

It's not so far-fetched when we have seen it in the movies. We've seen our own space shuttles flying around out there and the Hubble Space Telescope is sending back awesome views of our universe. I believe that we're being set up because the world is thinking something big is about to happen.

I've got a big event for you to think about: Suddenly, millions of people are going to one day vanish off the face of the Earth. You and I know I'm speaking of the Rapture of the church. But what about the guy who is left standing here? What context will he put the event in, especially when the greatest deceiver the world has ever known arises on the scene with all power and signs and lying wonders?

What are the people left in the world going to think, or be told, happened to all these people who have disappeared right in front of them? They might think these people have been transported into a spaceship with a transporter beam, just as if someone had commanded, "Beam me up, Scotty!"

How confused are we today about what's real and what isn't? Who knows anything for certain? NASA could say something and we'd say, "Okay, fine." In today's world, it seems, all we need is *plausibility*, not *possibility*. That's why *Jurassic Park* was so powerful, because people actually believe we have the technology to make it happen.

I've read a lot of writings by Stephen Hawking and some other astrophysicists. They fascinate me.

When I watch Star Trek, I realize that the writers weave real facts and theories into the story lines. So half of the plots are based on plausible possibilities and half on imagination. But we don't know which half is which unless we're an astrophysicist. The distinctions between fantasy and reality are becoming blurred.

This isn't just happening in the area of science. Much of our culture is influenced by television and movies. It's where we learn who's good and who's bad, what's right and what's wrong, what's evil and what's not, what's spiritual and what's carnal. The media defines these things for us if we allow them to be our only reference.

Now let's roll the clock back just a little here and say that
Bill Clinton is debating Bob Dole on television. Now let's
say that on another channel there's a debate about the same
issues, but it's between Jerry Seinfeld and Roseanne. What
do you think the ratings would be? A lot of people 35 and
under would watch Jerry and Roseanne because that's their
world. They want someone to make them laugh.

I saw a program about the U.S. presidential elections fea-
turing a couple of lawyers from the Libertarian Party, a guy
from the Democratic Party and Jason Alexander, who plays
George on Seinfeld. *Something is wrong with this picture.*
The attention turns to George and he is asked, "What do you
think the role of the government should be?"

He says, "Only one: free condom distribution!"

Then everybody roared at the joke because they realized
he wasn't trying to be serious. He's an actor. He was trying
to be funny. But why does he get national airtime to com-
ment about the political direction of the nation?

At one time, you could become a celebrity by doing
something heroic, or unique. Whether it was Winston
Churchill, or whoever, if you did something important that
made you a celebrity.

Now, however, you become a celebrity because you've
hired the right agent or because you've committed an out-
rageous or even a criminal act. Celebrity status today often
has nothing to do with worthwhile accomplishment. Look at
all the stories in magazines about lawyers who are on talk
shows. Using celebrities to speak out about issues has
become a means to an end.

In my opinion, the celebrity-making industry now *controls* the communication of the entire world through
movies and television. It sets the examples, not because of
the wisdom or intelligence of the these celebrities, but simply because they are famous.

In 1983, Jane Berne, who was the mayor of Chicago, ran for re-election. She wasn't very popular and about three or four weeks before the election she thought she should come up with a good strategy if she wanted to win. She hired an image consultant who changed her hair, her dress, her make-up and her walk. The consultant helped her soften her personal demeanor and they created commercials that revealed this new image to the voters. Suddenly, the mayor appeared to be soft-spoken, level-headed and responsible. She almost won the election!

Now, it would have been a better story if she did win. But the point is she almost won after being so disliked and unpopular, simply because of the image created by her image consultant. With three or four weeks of television ads, not reality, coming at them, a lot of people bought the new image, just like that.

Think of the power when the Antichrist arises in the world. This guy isn't going to be seen as evil. He's going to appear to be fabulous. All the world is going to eat up the great image he's portrayed as having.

I was just thinking of Princess Diana's funeral, and of how many people around the world watched it. In Toronto, Canada there is The Princess of Wales Theater, named after her a number of years ago. The flowers left in front of the theater practically blocked the street.

My wife Patti and I flipped on the TV just moments after the accident. We suddenly realized we were a part of one of the biggest global media events ever on television, bigger even than the O.J. Simpson trial.

The world was glued to the TV in the days following the accident and I recognized something happening in the media, something bigger than ever. What comes to mind, and I don't know how this passage of Scripture will be fulfilled, was the Scripture that says the Antichrist, this beloved man in the eyes of the world, will receive an apparently fatal head wound. I think the world on that day will definitely be glued to their TV sets. The Gulf War, the O.J. Simpson trial, and Diana's funeral were all dry runs for this future mega-media event.

If you want to think of some big events for a generation that's waiting for something big to happen, just start reading the Book of Revelation. This world is looking for something big and it is about to get it.

Let me return to the blurred lines between reality and fiction. Think about the famous "debate" between former Vice President Quayle and TV character Murphy Brown. Quayle was caught up in a "debate" on morality with a fictional character.

Murphy Brown made fun of Quayle's beliefs, and when he responded, the writers of the program had the character say, "He's an idiot, he's debating a fictional character." The writers made him look foolish.

But what was really taking place was a debate between Dan Quayle and the *writers* of Murphy Brown. And maybe Quayle even had writers for his speeches, too. So the behind the scenes, writers had their puppets on stage talking for them.

A survey a few years ago showed that about 80% of the articles we read in the newspaper are provided by the press agents of various companies and organizations.

So, for example, if you read an article saying that chocolate is good for weight loss, it's likely that the article was written by and based on a study conducted by a chocolate factory. Even when you're reading the newspaper now, it's hard to distinguish between what's real and what isn't. The lines have become blurred.

Our generation is poorly prepared to deal with the enormous issues that we confront. Yet we are the generation that is going to face some of the biggest issues because of the technology racing down the road. There isn't anything in history that can prepare us for what's taking place.

Maybe we're at the exact moment in history where technology and deception will come together. Think of virtual reality and the deceptive worlds it will be able to create. The technology exists. All that is needed is faster computers to drive it.

The world is set up for the fulfillment of prophecy. It's not just about earthquakes, famines and wars. We are seeing the prophesied deception being set up, which will counter reality.

While we don't know the day or the hour of the Lord's return, we can look at the signs of the times and know we are living right at the edge of it.

I don't care if it happens in the year 2000 or 2050; the important thing is that the signs are telling us this is the first generation that could see it happen. ∎

CHAPTER THIRTEEN

The Disappearance Of the Church

—by Arno Froese

Summary

We answer six basic questions about this well established Christian doctrine—the Blessed Hope of the church. The author blows away the smoke and false teachings to anchor the church in the assurance of the coming Rapture. Humble yourself before His countenance and ask Him to give you the grace to be ready at any moment!

*B*ehold, I shew you a mystery; We shall not all sleep, but we shall all be changed, In a moment, in the twinkling of an eye, at the last trump: for the trumpet shall sound, and the dead shall be raised incorruptible, and we shall be changed.

"For this corruptible must put on incorruption, and this mortal must put on immortality.

"So when this corruptible shall have put on incorruption, and this mortal shall have put on immortality, then shall be brought to pass the saying that is written, Death is swallowed up in victory" (1st Corinthians 15:51–54).

The above Scripture describes what we call "the Rapture." The word "Rapture," however, isn't found in the KJV English Bible translation.

Some have stated that the Rapture is an invention of man and is therefore not Biblical. In this message, however, we'll show that the Rapture is a reality clearly taught in the Scripture and that we can expect this climaxing event of the church to happen at any moment and without warning.

Because the word "Rapture" doesn't appear in our Bible doesn't mean it's not taught. The word "Trinity" isn't found in our Bible either, but the Trinity is clearly taught in the Scripture, even in the very first three verses:

God the Father: *"In the beginning God created the heaven and the Earth."*

God the Holy Spirit: *"And the Earth was without form, and void; and darkness was upon the face of the deep. And the spirit of God moved upon the face of the waters."*

God the Word [Son]: *"And God said, Let there be light: and there was light."* The Word is the Son of God, who has become flesh. In addition, we read in The New Testament in 1st John 5:7, *"For there are three that bear record in heaven, the Father, the Word, and the Holy Ghost: and these three are one."*

The Scripture we read at the beginning, 1st Corinthians 15, describes the Rapture in a crystal-clear manner. It talks about people who won't be "asleep," that means who won't die, and those who shall be changed in a twinkling of an eye. This changing process, or transfiguration, is basic; otherwise, the Rapture for those who are alive then is a non-event.

The Bible says flesh and blood can't inherit the kingdom of God. Thus, a change must happen. We can confirm with perfect assurance that such an event has never taken place in the church's history. Verse 54 particularly highlights this fact when it says, "...*then shall be brought to pass the saying that is written, Death is swallowed up in victory.*" For almost 2,000 years now, members of the church have been dying physically. Millions upon millions of saints have died.

If the Lord delays His coming this year, millions more will experience this death. The Bible says "...*it is appointed unto men once to die...*" (Hebrews 9:27). But 1st Corinthians 15:54 very clearly says that death will be swallowed up in victory. That, we all have to admit, hasn't happened yet, but will happen at the time of the Rapture.

Let me explain the Rapture by answering six questions:

1. *What* is the Rapture?

2. *Why* is the Rapture necessary?

3. *How* will the Rapture take place?

4. *Who* will be raptured?

5. *When* will the Rapture take place?

6. *How* should we prepare for the Rapture?

1. What Is the Rapture?

The Rapture is the final fulfillment of the resurrection and the ascension of our Lord Jesus. He is the head; we are the body. We must be united!

The Rapture is also the answer to Jesus' prayer in John 17:24, *"Father, I will that they also, whom thou hast given me, be with me where I am; that they may behold my glory, which thou hast given me: for thou lovedst me before the foundation of the world."*

This is the Lord's clear expressed will—that His own, which He has bought with His precious blood, be with Him in His presence so they finally may behold His glory!

The Rapture is the transformation into the image of Him who was transformed before us: *"Beloved, now are we the sons of God, and it doth not yet appear what we shall be: but we know that, when he shall appear, we shall be like him; for we shall see him as he is"* (1st John 3:2). We can rightly say the Rapture is fulfillment of Bible prophecy!

2. Why Is the Rapture Necessary?

Let me highlight five important points:

A. *The Rapture is necessary to permit sin to reach its climax.* The church is the Light of the world, so sin can't fully develop. Here's an example in the Old Testament: When God gave the promise to Abraham regarding the Promised Land, He said, *"But in the fourth generation they shall come hither again: for the iniquity of the Amorites is not yet full"* (Genesis 15:16). God is righteous. He couldn't punish the Amorites at that time because their measure of sin hadn't been fulfilled. After they had reached the limit, God used Israel as the tool of judgment to destroy that nation.

God can't send destructive judgment upon the world because the measure of sin hasn't been fulfilled yet. But this full measure of sin can't happen because the hindering element for the fulfillment of sin is the Light of the world, which lives in the church.

Someone may now object and say, "The world is in such a terrible mess and people are so sinful, corrupt, and immoral that God can't permit this to continue."

No doubt, there's an increase of evil as prophesied in 2nd Timothy 3:13, *"But evil men and seducers shall wax worse and worse, deceiving, and being deceived."*

But to see the climax of evil, we must look at the Scripture that describes the time when the church is gone. After the sixth seal is opened, we read in Revelation 6:15–16, *"And the kings of the earth, and the great men, and the rich men, and the chief captains, and the mighty men, and every bondman, and every free man, hid themselves in the dens and in the rocks of the mountains;*

"And said to the mountains and rocks, Fall on us, and hide us from the face of him that sitteth on the throne, and from the wrath of the Lamb."

Despite such terrible threat and destruction which is coming upon them, they find no room for repentance. Instead they try to hide themselves from the wrath of the Lamb.

But that's not all. Revelation 9:20–21 reads, *"And the rest of the men which were not killed by these plagues yet repented not of the works of their hands, that they should not worship devils, and idols of gold, and silver, and brass, and stone, and of wood: which neither can see, nor hear, nor walk:*

"Neither repented they of their murders, nor of their sorceries, nor of their fornication, nor of their thefts."

Even after one-third of mankind is killed, these people can find no room for repentance.

It gets worse. Revelation 16 describes the most horrible judgment upon mankind, yet we read, *"And men were scorched with great heat, and blasphemed the name of God, which hath power over these plagues: and they repented not to give him glory.*

"And the fifth angel poured out his vial upon the seat of the beast; and his kingdom was full of darkness; and they gnawed their tongues for pain,

"And blasphemed the God of heaven because of their pains and their sores, and repented not of their deeds" (verses 9–11). Not only did they not repent, but they blasphemed the name of God.

B. *The Rapture is necessary to allow the Antichrist to be revealed.* The highest product of darkness is the Antichrist. He can take his rightful place only when the church has been removed. The prince of darkness can't fully develop his diabolical plan while the church is present. Jesus said, *"Ye are the light of the world..."* (Matthew 5:14).

The Apostle Paul, when speaking about the coming of the Lord Jesus Christ to Earth and our "gathering unto Him," which is the Rapture, clearly identifies in verse 6 and 7 of 2nd Thessalonians chapter two, the hindering element which is the Holy Spirit in the church, *"And now ye know what withholdeth that he might be revealed in his time.*

"For the mystery of iniquity doth already work: only he who now letteth will let, until he be taken out of the way." The Holy Spirit convicts the world of sin but also lives in the believer. Jesus testifies, *"...I will pray the Father, and he shall give you another Comforter, that he may abide with you for ever"* (John 14:16).

Few Christians fully realize the meaning of being bornagain: We're a dwelling place of the Holy Spirit! The mystery of iniquity can never completely enlarge its work of darkness as long as there's one spark of light present on Earth. What happens when the Holy Spirit, with the church, is taken out of the way? The next verse gives the answer,

"...then shall that wicked be revealed...." Surely, no one can argue the fact that the mystery of iniquity is already at work, especially in our day as we see the whole world collectively turning away from the living God and embracing the secular psychological view of "self-esteem."

Is the Rapture needed? From this point of view, we realize it's a necessity that we're taken out of the way.

C. *The Rapture is necessary for the initiation of the casting out of Satan from heaven.* How do you know Satan is in heaven? We find the answer in Revelation 12:10 where it says, *"...for the accuser of our brethren is cast down, which accused them before our God day and night."*

Who is he "accusing"? Not Israel, not the world, but the "brethren" who are bought with the precious blood of the Lord!

These brethren who are on Earth live in their "tabernacle" of flesh and blood, which can't inherit the kingdom of God; thus these born-again believers are subject unto sin. We're redeemed from the *power* of sin and from the *guilt* of sin but not from the *presence* of sin.

Therefore, when sin is committed, the Devil has a legitimate claim against us. But praise God; that's not the end, for we have a lawyer, an advocate in heaven, the High Priest who makes intercession for us!

The moment you and I commit a sin, we come under the judgment of the Scripture, *"He that committeth sin is of the devil...."* Subsequently, Satan has a right to stand before God and accuse us.

But when we recognize our sins and confess them to our Lord, the High Priest becomes active and stands before God contradicting Satan, saying in effect, "I have bought this person with my precious blood. Therefore, it is forgiven, paid in full!"

The casting out of Satan from heaven is preceded by a battle, *"And there was war in heaven: Michael and his angels fought against the dragon; and the dragon fought and his angels,*

"And prevailed not; neither was their place found any more in heaven.

"And the great dragon was cast out, that old serpent, called the devil, and Satan, which deceiveth the whole world: he was cast out into the earth, and his angels were cast out with him" (Revelation 12:7–9).

This casting out is also needed because the church is being raptured into heaven, and Satan has lost his job. Why did he lose his job? Because there's no one left to accuse!

He doesn't have to accuse the world because he is in charge; he actually is "the god of this world"! The Earth's inhabitants are the children of darkness who follow in the footsteps of the prince of this world. Satan is cast upon the Earth and now will successfully control mankind because the light is *"taken out of the way."* Revelation 12:12 summarizes the contrast between these two groups, *"Therefore rejoice, ye heavens, and ye that dwell in them. Woe to the inhabiters of the earth and of the sea! for the devil is come down unto you, having great wrath, because he knoweth that he hath but a short time."*

D. *The Rapture is necessary because the Word of God must be fulfilled.* When the Apostle Paul wrote to the Corinthians and showed to them the mystery of the Rapture, he said, *"So when this corruptible shall have put on incorruption, and this mortal shall have put on immortality, then shall be brought to pass the saying that is written, Death is swallowed up in victory"* (1st Corinthians 15:54).

Although Jesus has defeated the powers of Satan and death on Calvary's cross, His victory over death hasn't been transferred to His body, the church. We, similar to anyone else, must die. For almost 2,000 years, the saints have died, and have been buried in the grave.

Here, we have another prophetic pointer to the Rapture; namely, our similitude of being buried with the Lord. For two millennia, the saints have been buried—not translated —waiting for the fulness of the body so the whole church can be raised in the twinkling of an eye to meet her Lord in the air. Only when the church is raptured, *"...then shall be brought to pass the saying that is written, Death is swallowed up in victory."* Only then is the body united with the head, who is the fulness of the Godhead.

E. *The Rapture is necessary so we can come back and judge the world.* Paul wrote to the Corinthians, *"Do ye not know that the saints shall judge the world..."* (1st Corinthians 6:2). It's impossible for us to judge the world now because we're not perfected. We're still in our sinful flesh and blood. Our judgment would fail to fulfill the righteousness of God because even a saved sinner can't judge righteously.

This, incidentally, is an added confirmation that exposes the vain effort of some believers to install a righteous government in our nation, or for that matter, in any nation in the world. Such a promise hasn't been given unto us and therefore, any effort, no matter how well intended, is doomed.

3. How Will the Rapture Take Place?
It will take place in the twinkling of an eye, instantly, suddenly, unannounced, with no warning or time given for people to prepare for it.

It is of utmost importance that we first learn to distinguish our Rapture from the Rapture of the Jews. We'll be raptured vertically, from Earth to heaven; the Jews will be raptured horizontally, from the four corners of the Earth to Israel.

Our meeting place is clearly described in 1st Thessalonians 4:17, *"...in the air...."* The Jewish Rapture will lead to the land of Israel. God has given them an unconditional promise that He will return them to their land, *"...I have gathered them into their own land and have left none of them anymore there"* (Ezekiel 39:28).

The Vertical Rapture

Let's read the two Scriptures describing these two Raptures so we'll not confuse them. The Rapture of the church is described in 1st Corinthians 15:51–53, *"Behold, I shew you a mystery; We shall not all sleep, but we shall all be changed,*

"In a moment, in the twinkling of an eye, at the last trump: for the trumpet shall sound, and the dead shall be raised incorruptible, and we shall be changed.

"For this corruptible must put on incorruption, and this mortal must put on immortality."

And, in 1st Thessalonians 4:16–17, we read *"For the Lord himself shall descend from heaven with a shout, with the voice of the archangel, and with the trump of God: and the dead in Christ shall rise first:*

"Then we which are alive and remain shall be caught up together with them in the clouds, to meet the Lord in the air: and so shall we ever be with the Lord."

This is crystal clear: We will meet the Lord by moving UP.

The Horizontal Rapture

The Rapture of the Jews to Israel is described in Matthew 24:31, *"And he shall send his angels with a great sound of a trumpet, and they shall gather together his elect from the four winds, from one end of heaven to the other."* Here, we do well to explain that Jesus is speaking to His people, the

Jews, and not to the church. In this well-known chapter, Matthew 24, we see a geographical note in verse 16, *"Then let them which be in Judaea flee into the mountains."* You can't apply this to the church.

Furthermore, verse 24 mentions the "Sabbath day" which is given exclusively to the Jewish people. *"It is a sign between me and the children of Israel for ever..."* (Exodus 31:17).

Now let's compare these two events.

The Lord Himself and His Angels

At the Rapture of the church we read, *"...the Lord himself shall descend from heaven...."* But in Matthew 24:31 we read, *"...He shall send his angels...."*

For the church, He comes *"...with the voice of the archangel and with the trump of God."*

For Israel, He comes with *"a trumpet."*

These distinctive descriptions show the difference between these two Raptures: one for the church and the other for the Jews. *One* will lead to the clouds in the heavens, and the *other* will lead to Jerusalem!

We must realize that it's impossible for the Scripture to be fulfilled which says that the Jews will *"...look upon me [Jesus] whom they have pierced..."* (Zechariah 12:10) if the Jews aren't back in Israel! The return of the Jews to the land of Israel, which we're witnessing today, is part of the fulfillment of Bible prophecy. But, it will *climax* in the instantaneous removal of the entire remaining remnant to the land of their fathers. Not one will be left behind. All will be raptured to the land of Israel!

The "Trump of God" And "A Trumpet"

We noticed that Israel will be gathered with "a trump," but the church with "the trump of God."

Let's explore this specific difference and reread the description of 1st Corinthians 15, where it says in verse 52, *"...at the last trump...."* The Rapture of the church, therefore, will happen at the last trump of God. This trumpet must not be confused with any other trumpet, such as trumps of angels, trumps of priests, trumps of peace and trumps of war, or the trumpets we read about in the Book of Revelation, announcing terrible judgment upon the world. We're dealing here with "the last trump of God." Thus, a natural question arises: "Where is the *first* trump of God?"

Here, we must read Exodus 19:16, *"And it came to pass on the third day in the morning, that there were thunders and lightnings, and a thick cloud upon the mount, and the voice of the trumpet exceeding loud; so that all the people that was in the camp trembled."* Note: We have the "voice" and the "trumpet." We can search the Scriptures from Genesis to Revelation and won't find the presence of the Lord identified with the "voice" of a "trumpet" anywhere else.

Let's also read verse 19 to reenforce the identity of the trumpet, God, and the voice, *"And when the voice of the trumpet sounded long, and waxed louder and louder, Moses spake, and God answered him by a voice."*

What was the purpose of this event? The gathering of His people to hear God's Word!

There's no proof in the Scripture that the sound of the first trump of God was heard by anyone but those in the camp of Israel.

Likewise, the *last* trump of God won't be noticed by the world, but will be heard only by those who have the inner spiritual ear, that is, the born-again believers. Remember Jesus saying repeatedly to the seven churches in Revelation, *"He that hath an ear, let him hear what the Spirit saith unto the churches."* What is the purpose of the last trump of God?

To gather His heavenly people to receive the Word which has become flesh!

The Third Day
In the event recorded for us in Exodus, we also see a prophetic pointer to the resurrection of our Lord Jesus, *"And be ready against the third day: for the third day the Lord will come down in the sight of all the people upon mount Sinai"* (Exodus 19:11).

The third day is of tremendous importance because our Lord arose *on* the third day, not as often is assumed, mistakenly, that He arose *after* the third day. Two disciples testify on the evening of the third day, *"But we trusted that it had been he which should have redeemed Israel: and beside all this, today is the third day since these things were done"* (Luke 24:21). Isn't it important, then, to realize we're approaching the third day? With the Lord, a thousand years is as one day and one day as a thousand years. Our Lord has been gone for almost two days and the third day is rapidly approaching!

4. Who Will Be Raptured?
We don't find proof in the Scripture stating that the Rapture is a *reward* or our *inheritance*. The Rapture is the result, based on the exclusive work of our Lord Jesus Christ, proving the power of His resurrection in His body. We must conclude, therefore, that *all* born-again believers will be raptured. We're the body of Christ!

In addition, it's evident from the Scriptures which we've read describing the Rapture that the Apostle Paul, inspired by the Holy Spirit, uses the word "we" and "us" repeatedly when He speaks of those who will be raptured.

Surely, had he meant otherwise, he would have written, "They who are ready..." or "Those who have achieved a certain spiritual standard..." but that's *not* what he wrote.

Specifically, in 1st Corinthians 15, when He speaks about the mystery, He says *"...we shall not all sleep but we shall all be changed."* Similarly, we read the "we" twice in verse 17 of 1st Thessalonians 4.

Then, in chapter 5 of 1st Thessalonians, Paul draws the distinction concerning those who will *not* be raptured, but will be left behind, *"For when they shall say, Peace and safety; then sudden destruction cometh upon them, as travail upon a woman with child; and they shall not escape."* Please note the words, "they," and "them."

A moment later, in verses 4–6, He describes the church, *"But ye, brethren, are not in darkness, that that day should overtake you as a thief. Ye are all the children of light, and the children of the day: we are not of the night, nor of darkness.*

"Therefore let us not sleep, as do others; but let us watch and be sober." The words, "we" and "us" reinforces the clear division.

5. When Will the Rapture Take Place?

Here, we must emphasize strongly that all speculations are fundamentally wrong. They've been wrong in the past and will continue to be wrong in the future. The Scripture plainly states, *"Be ye therefore ready also: for the Son of man cometh at an hour when ye think not"* (Luke 12:40).

Date Setting

Much damage has been done by those who have tried to pinpoint a date of the Lord's return. Without exception, all have been false prophets. No doubt, those prophets have done great harm to the Church of Jesus Christ and the proclamation of the prophetic Word.

In 1988, a retired NASA space engineer named Edgar Whisenant wrote a book, *88 Reasons Why The Rapture*

Could Take Place In 1988. The book was well-written and well-researched, but it was also well-wrong!

During that time, our office was flooded with telephone calls by questioning believers. We were asked what our position was regarding such a prediction. My answer always was, "Jesus will come at an hour when we think not"!

The biggest problem with any prediction is the fact that by pinpointing a date, the element of surprise is taken from the Scripture.

Throughout the Bible, we read about the absolute requirement of being ready at any time. Therefore, if someone takes it upon himself to predict that the Lord will come in five days, it means, in practical terms, "I don't have to wait for Him today or tomorrow, because He'll come on the fifth day!" Such a teaching violates the Holy Scripture and therefore must be outrightly rejected.

I'm reminded of an elderly rabbi in Jerusalem who one day was interrupted by a young student who excitedly reported to him that he had figured out, from the Torah, the day of the coming of the Messiah. This young man said, "The Messiah will come on the Sabbath!"

But the old rabbi replied, "Son, I don't believe you because I'm waiting for Him to come today!"

Mid-Tribulation Rapture?
Someone may now ask, "Is it possible that the Rapture can happen in the middle of the Tribulation?" My answer is "No." Why? Because the Tribulation is made possible by the absence of the church. The church is the Light of the world and the deceptive work of Satan can't climax while the church is still present. The mid-Tribulation theory also violates the Scripture regarding the surprise element. You can't take away the surprise element. It's in the Word of God, and you can't eliminate it.

To believe in the mid-Tribulation Rapture, you must ignore many Scriptures, including Titus 2:13, *"Looking for that blessed hope, and the glorious appearing of the great God and our Saviour Jesus Christ."* When you believe in the mid-Tribulation Rapture, you definitely can't wait for Jesus today, but you're actually waiting for the beginning of the Tribulation and the appearance of the Antichrist. Such teaching, however, is contrary to the Scriptures. Again, we may search the Bible from Genesis to Revelation, but won't find any admonition anywhere that we should be looking for the coming of the Tribulation!

Post-Tribulation Rapture?
What about the possibility of the Rapture happening after the Great Tribulation? To such a question, we give an even more emphatic "No"! Not only is this contrary to the Scripture, but it's impossible because *no one would be left to be raptured!*

The only way to become a believer in the Tribulation period is to die for it! From Revelation 13:15, we read: *"And he had power to give life unto the image of the Beast, that the image of the Beast should both speak, and cause that as many as would not worship the image of the Beast should be killed."*

A born-again believer, when faced with the alternative, will never deny his Lord by bowing down to the image of the Beast and worshipping it!

Someone may now say, "But won't there be many who will be afraid to lose their life, later deny the Lord, and worship the image of the Beast?" I'm convinced that it can't happen.

In times of great need and severe persecution, the Lord gives the needed grace for His saints to lay down their lives for Him. We have adequate proof in the Scripture as well as numerous examples throughout the history of Christianity. But this is a pointless debate because we've already seen that the Great Tribulation can't happen unless the church is taken out of the way, because the absence of the church is the reason for the Great Tribulation.

6. How Should We Prepare For the Rapture?

First, you must be born-again. Without the rebirth, you'll remain in total darkness, without hope, and lost for all eternity. John 3:36 testifies, *"He that believeth on the Son hath everlasting life: and he that believeth not the Son shall not see life; but the wrath of God abideth on him."*

The person without Christ is in total darkness and shall not see life. To the religious Pharisee, Nicodemus, Jesus said, *"...Verily, verily I say unto thee, except a man be born-again, he cannot see the kingdom of God."* Therefore, if you're not born-again, you'll be left behind.

This moment, as you read these lines, may be your last chance to come to Jesus for the forgiveness of your sins and to receive eternal life.

The way to become a believer in Jesus is simple: Trust and accept that He is the Son of God who has poured out His blood on Calvary's cross for your sins. Turn away from them and accept His free pardon. That guarantees you eternal life. I urge you, therefore, to make this decision today, even at this very hour. I can't help you, nor can your pastor or anyone else. You need to go to Jesus and ask Him to make you His child. The Son of God promises, *"...him that cometh to me I will in no wise cast out"* (John 6:37).

Unfortunately, the term "rebirth" has been popularized, and frequently, people don't understand the full meaning of it. How can you be sure you're born-again? Let's list seven steps for a newborn Christian. Consider an example: A little baby has just been born. What does he do?

First, He cries! That means when you're born-again, you'll begin to cry to God; you'll start praying.

Second, the baby eats. Why? Because he's hungry. You'll hunger for the Word of God, not because you have to, but because you want to. Reading the Word of God is your spiritual food.

Third, the baby learns to listen. You'll begin to heed the Word of God and take His commandments seriously.

Fourth, the baby thrives on interaction with others. Christian fellowship is important for you. You'll become active in a local church where you serve the Lord in fellowship with other believers.

Fifth, as the baby grows into young adulthood, he becomes increasingly aware. You'll become more aware of the fact that you're a sinner saved by grace, and because of that, you'll seek your progressive sanctification; that is, you'll aim to be an ever-more-effective servant for His purposes.

Sixth, as you grow through the youthful stage, you will look to the future. As a born-again person, you'll want to *know* the future as well, and you'll begin to study the prophetic Word, which tells you all about it. God's invitation is, *"...Ask me of things to come...."* (Isaiah 45:11).

Seventh, as a young adult matures, he strives toward goals. As a Christian, the goal is His coming, for He's our beginning and end; He's the author of our salvation, and desiring His return is natural.

First Corinthians 1:7 confirms, *"So that ye come behind in no gift; waiting for the coming of our Lord Jesus Christ."* That means this gift of waiting for Him must be a reality in your life.

As we grow older, we realize that our time on Earth is limited. Thus, there will be an increased wish for the coming of the Lord. Let's confirm this with several Scriptures,

"Looking for that blessed hope, and the glorious appearing of the great God and our Saviour Jesus Christ" (Titus 2:13). That's looking for the Rapture!

Hebrews 9:28 reinforces this, *"So Christ was once offered to bear the sins of many; and unto them that look for him shall he appear the second time without sin unto salvation."*

Our Duty and Our Hope

Not only are we to look; we're also to wait, especially in view of the coming Great Tribulation, which is the wrath of God, *"And to wait for his Son from heaven, whom he raised from the dead, even Jesus, which delivered us from the wrath to come"* (1st Thessalonians 1:10).

While we look and wait, we're also instructed to be patient. Here James admonishes us urgently, *"Be patient therefore, brethren, unto the coming of the Lord. Behold, the husbandman waiteth for the precious fruit of the earth, and hath long patience for it, until he receive the early and latter rain.*

"Be ye also patient; stablish your hearts: for the coming of the Lord draweth nigh" (James 5:7–8).

This patient looking and waiting for Him gives us the additional strength and courage to go forward in His work, even increasing as the days proceed.

When the Apostle Paul wrote to the Corinthians about the Rapture, he ended that message with an important admonition, *"Therefore, my beloved brethren, be ye stedfast, unmoveable, always abounding in the work of the Lord, forasmuch as ye know that your labour is not in vain in the Lord"* (1st Corinthians 15:58).

To the Thessalonians, after writing about the Rapture, he said, *"Comfort your hearts, and stablish you in every good word and work"* (2nd Thessalonians 2:17).

And in 1st Thessalonians 4:18, he ends the description of the Rapture with, *"Wherefore comfort one another with these words."*

It's my sincere prayer that the Lord will comfort you with the hope of the coming Rapture and by that you'll increase in the work of the Lord in these endtimes. How much time we have left, I don't know, but based on the developments in Israel and the world, we recognize that the approach of the end stages of the endtime is near. Therefore, *"...To day if ye will hear his voice,*

"Harden not your hearts, as in the provocation, in the day of temptation in the wilderness" (Hebrews 3:7–8).

Humble yourself before His countenance and ask Him to give you the grace to be ready at any moment! ■

Arno Froese is the Executive Director of Midnight Call Ministries located in Columbia, South Carolina, and founder of a new publishing division, *The Olive Press*.

He is Executive Editor of *Midnight Call* and *News From Israel*, which are published in numerous languages.

Froese has authored hundreds of magazine features. His latest books, *How Democracy Will Elect the Antichrist*, and *Saddam's Mystery Babylon*, are well received by an ever-increasing audience.

He has hosted nearly 50 national and international Bible conferences.

In addition, Mr. Froese is host of the monthly Message Of the Month Club, a Video Club, and regularly leads study tours to Israel.

His international outlook and unique insight have earned him a position on the platform with the most well-known Bible authorities in this generation.

Peter Lalonde is one of the brightest personalities today presenting the endtime message that Jesus is coming soon. He especially appeals to the younger generation by referring to technology they are familiar with, such as computers and virtual reality, showing how they relate to Bible prophecy.

Along with his brother Paul, and wife Patti, he directs *This Week in Bible Prophecy*, one of the most highly-rated ministries on Christian television across North America. Success on television has led him to full-scale feature movie production, which includes his latest release, *Apocalypse*.

Peter Lalonde is also a prolific author as well, with releases including *One World Under Antichrist, 2000 A.D. Are You Ready?, Left Behind, 301 Startling Proofs For the Existence of God, The Edge Of Time, Racing Toward the Mark Of the Beast,* and the book version of *Apocalypse*.

D ave Hunt, without question, is one of the top Bible apologists of our generation. His fearless defense of the Biblical faith has earned him the unsolicited top spot on the *persona non grata* list of evolutionists, religious deceivers, occultists, false teachers and prophets, and apostate "Christian" churches, such as Roman Catholicism.

Dave Hunt's bestseller, *The Seduction Of Christianity*, exposed un-Biblical teaching that had taken hold within the church virtually unopposed.

His prolific writings, appearances on television, radio, video, cassettes, and conference engagements, have all kept the church alert to deceptive teachings that threaten to mislead the flock.

His books include *A Cup Of Trembling, Global Peace and the Rise of Antichrist, In Defense Of the Faith, Occult Invasion, Whatever Happened To Heaven, A Woman Rides the Beast, Peace, Prosperity and the Coming Holocaust* and others.

Alexander Seibel is a theologian with impressive ability to analyze the original Greek language of the New Testament.

He holds a Master of Technology degree and works full-time as an evangelist, speaking to students on science, the Bible, and evolution versus creation. He uncovers unhealthy trends in churches and society, pointing out un-Biblical practices, and recommending a Bible-based approach.

He has written several books, some of which have sold up to five editions. Several books are available in multiple languages.

The undeniable fulfillment of Biblical prophecies in relation to Israel softened his heart toward Christianity, he testifies, finally surrendering his life to Christ on August 4th, 1968, when he listened to a message about true discipleship.

Alexander Seibel, born in Austria, now lives in Germany, is married and the father of three children.

M oody Adams is a senior traveling evangelist, working along-
side some of the top ministers
in the Christian world. Moody is a well-
rounded and highly sought-after speaker,
fluent on any number of Bible topics,
and inspires his listeners and readers to
give their entire lives to Christ.

His audiocassettes, videos, and publi-
cations address a variety of topics which
are important for the Christian church
today as it faces a new opportunity.

In addition to a full-time traveling
speaking schedule in churches, Dr.
Adams appears on the conference platform with leading authorities in Bible
prophecy.

Some of his latest books and videos
include *Farrakhan, Islam, and the
Religion That Is Raping America*, and
the international best-seller *The Titanic's
Last Hero* which tells the emotionally
and spiritually challenging story of
Pastor John Harper, who went down with
the Titanic on that fateful night in 1912.

TOWARD THE SEVENTH MILLENNIUM

D r. David Webber is the author of several books, including *666: The MARK Is Ready*, and *The Image Of the Ages*. His newsletter, *Dave Webber Reports*, keeps readers informed monthly on prophetic topics.

Dr. Webber has been engaged in radio and television ministry for virtually his entire career across nearly 50 years. He has conducted radio interviews with nearly every notable Bible prophecy speaker.

Dr. Webber was formerly the principal speaker on the nationwide *Southwest Radio Church*, founded by his father, Rev. E.F. Webber.

Dr. Webber can often be seen at Bible prophecy conferences, a movement which he had a part in pioneering decades ago, and has travelled extensively on tours to Israel, the Middle East, and Russia. He is a well-known dean of Bible prophecy studies.

John Cionci, M.D., is a Philadelphia native, a graduate of Central H.S., the University of Pennsylvania, and the Philadelphia College of Osteopathic Medicine. He is a member of the American Osteopathic Association and Chair of the AIDS Committee for the Pennsylvania Osteopathic Medical Association.

Dr. Cionci has been a practicing physician since 1950. Semi-retired in 1988, he has dedicated his retirement to serving people with AIDS and educating the public about this disease.

As a born-again believer, Dr. Cionci is the author of hundreds of articles that give counsel to those involved with AIDS, and renders timely updates on the advances being made in AIDS treatment, always with a Christian admonition that Jesus is the only answer.

He has proven himself a highly accurate predictor of the global spread of AIDS and related diseases in the midst of the *politically compromised* debate.